Parents Make
the Difference

Parents Make the Difference

Nourishing Literacy Development through Shared Book Reading

Susan Voorhees

ROWMAN & LITTLEFIELD
Lanham • Boulder • New York • Toronto • Plymouth, UK

Published by Rowman & Littlefield
4501 Forbes Boulevard, Suite 200, Lanham, Maryland 20706
www.rowman.com

10 Thornbury Road, Plymouth PL6 7PP, United Kingdom

British Library Cataloguing in Publication Information Available

Library of Congress Cataloging-in-Publication Data
Voorhees, Susan, 1961–
  Parents make the difference : nourishing literacy development through shared book reading / Susan Voorhees.
     pages cm
  Includes bibliographical references.
  ISBN 978-1-4758-0321-1 (pbk. : alk. paper) — ISBN 978-1-4758-0322-8 (electronic)
  1. Reading (Early childhood)—Parent participation. I. Title.
  LB1139.5.R43V66 2014
  372.4—dc23
                                                                              2014006101

∞™ The paper used in this publication meets the minimum requirements of American National Standard for Information Sciences—Permanence of Paper for Printed Library Materials, ANSI/NISO Z39.48-1992.

Printed in the United States of America

Dedicated in memory of my mother—
my first teacher

Contents

FINAL THOUGHTS

Preface

Young children are complex, literate human beings. Just sit and watch pre-schoolers interact for a few minutes with their environment; you can almost see their minds developing as if you were watching through the lens of a time-lapse camera. Given any situation, young children naturally problem solve as they navigate everyday interactions, making sense of the world around them as they develop literacy competence and performance.

Parents are natural facilitators of their children's literacy development. Parents create all sorts of daily home and community routines that provide a positive and effective influence on their youngsters' literacy learning. Grand-parents or other consistent caretakers are equally important and often provide the same types of literacy activities. Today, it is common knowledge in the education field that there is a very strong connection between the home environment and children's language and literacy development.

However, I first learned of this connection when I was just completing my undergraduate degree, in 1983. This is when an educator by the name of Denny Taylor first came up with the term *family literacy* based on her three-year study observing six families with young children who were successfully learning to read and write. Family literacy can be defined as the different ways parents, caretakers, and extended family engage in authentic literacy activities at home and in the community (Morrow, Paratore, and Tracey 1994). These home literacy practices might include something as simple as using lists for grocery shopping to the more sophisticated activity of shared book reading. This is when parents or other caretakers read aloud to children; sometimes it is referred to as *lap reading*. The concept of *family literacy* caught the attention of many educators, including me, as Dr. Taylor and many others continued to expand on this field of study for many, many years to come.

My first teaching position after completing my undergraduate degree was as a kindergarten teacher, and I naturally began to relate the ideas of *family literacy* to my observations and interactions with my school children and their parents. The variation in my kindergarteners' literacy development was vast. On one end of the spectrum, there were students like Suzanne; she was already conventionally reading and viewed herself as a reader. Suzanne loved story time and any other literacy activity. On the other end, there were children like Alison; she seemed to struggle and stress over learning the letters of the alphabet. From the very beginning of the year, Alison was disengaged during story time, and certainly, she didn't view herself as competent when it came to any literacy tasks.

Additionally, some of my parents were very involved; other parents not so much, but almost every parent asked me the age-old question, "How can I help my child learn to read?" I gave what had become, and still is, the universal response, "Read to them." Yet, even back then, I felt this was inadequate; I have always believed this question from parents needed to be given a more thoughtful, detailed response than a perfunctory three-word answer. Parents and their children deserved more. Yet, at that time, I didn't have further recommendations to offer.

This feeling of inadequacy in my response lingered, and as I continued my graduate work in literacy education, and then began my doctoral studies in reading, language, and cognition, I would often share my displeasure with my peers about this three-word answer to parents. Finally one day, my doctoral professor abruptly interrupted me and said, "You now have the knowledge; you should stop complaining and do something about it. . . . Start providing workshops for parents as reading partners." And so I did.

At first, I was unsure about how well I would be received by the parents during these workshops, but I quickly found that parents have a thirst for literacy knowledge. What better motivator was there than for parents to understand how to guide their children to become life-long readers? So my workshops addressed many complex concepts. My goals included increasing parents' understanding of reading, introducing parents to book reading techniques and strategies for both narrative and informational text, and connecting reading practices with state and national standards. The parents easily grasped these ideas, and I believed I was making a difference. The possibilities were endless as I engaged in parent education.

Very interested in the early years of literacy development, I also decided to write my dissertation about parents' behaviors during shared book reading and how their behaviors affect their young children's reading development. My research documented how parents' beliefs about reading influenced their reading practices with their children. In turn, their children were predisposed to having the same reading beliefs and practices. It was amazing to see such similarities. As a literacy-education professor for the past sixteen years, in each of my courses, I have continued to promote the important role of parents and the influence they have on their children.

From the beginning of life, parents provide nourishment to their children and teach them good health habits to prevent later health problems. This same thinking should follow for literacy development. Language and literacy development begin from the first day a child is born. If children are not provided with appropriate language and literacy experiences from the beginning, they are at risk of being cognitively and affectively *malnourished.*

I've provided reading intervention for many children who had not developed effective reading behaviors, but I found the longer children practice poor habits, the more challenging it is to help them. These children do not identify themselves as readers because they have been unsuccessful for years. The key point of this book is that it is far more effective and inspiring to nurture young children's literacy development than to rely on reading intervention later on in their lives. This book is about a proactive *response to prevention* to avoid later reading intervention. Early-childhood-education teachers are responsible for part of children's literacy nourishment, but parents are equally responsible.

Twenty-six years ago, I gave birth to my daughter. I remember the nurse handing my little one to me, and just as I began to coddle her lovingly in my arms, my new mother jitters began. It was at that moment that I realized that, as her parent, I was also her teacher. I was her first teacher, and I would probably have the greatest influence on who she became as she grew and developed. I can remember getting a migraine headache the day I left the hospital as my anxiety grew. The nurse gave me a long list of instructions, and my family and friends provided a ton of *unsolicited* advice. (It was no wonder I had a migraine!) It was that day that I realized being a parent was an enormous responsibility.

I don't think there is a parent reading this who doesn't understand that parenting involves a multitude of roles! Through the years, I've had days when I've felt like a skilled parent, and days when I've had my follies. An immediate memory that comes to mind is the first time I forgot to strap my daughter into her high chair, and she came crashing down onto the kitchen floor. She wasn't hurt—thank goodness. So, I wouldn't even think of giving you advice on general parenting; however, I would like to guide you in fostering your children's literacy development, my area of expertise.

This book is, therefore, an invitation to all parents of young children; as shareholders of your children's literacy development, this book will inform you on how to best read to your children as a preventative measure against future literacy and academic problems. It will clearly explain to you how to effectively engage in one of the most important family literacy activities, that is, shared book reading. It is not my purpose to teach parents how to teach reading; one would need to complete a master's degree in literacy education to achieve this goal, but it will guide you to nourish your children's literacy development as they naturally move toward learning to read and become *lovers* of reading. It is my pleasure to share some sound advice with you.

Think of this book as an early childhood literacy education workshop for parents. It is quite possible, that you, the parent, will in fact make the greatest difference in your child's early literacy success, and I promise, reading this book will not give you a migraine headache! Welcome.

—Susan Voorhees

Acknowledgments

Conversation surrounding the ideas of literacy with family, friends, parents, educators, and colleagues has been my greatest instructional tool, and therefore, there are many people who contributed to who I am today as a literate being. While I cannot identify all of them, I would like to acknowledge several people who provided insight and impacted my thinking as a literacy educator, specifically in the area of early childhood education. They were my inspiration in completing this book project.

I would like to thank two of my dear colleagues and longtime friends, Karen Cirincione and Linda Bausch. The pure passion Karen displays in believing that shared book reading is the greatest gift parents, grandparents, and teachers can give to young children has been and continues to be my motivation. She has always brought me back to my *roots* as to why I became a literacy educator. Likewise, Linda always energizes (and re-energizes) me as a literacy educator. Her encouragement through our many e-mail and in-person conversations has been invaluable in completing this project.

Thank you to my childhood friend, Mary Bettenhauser, who as a pre-school teacher for many years, has contributed to my understanding about what parents and preschool teachers need to know and how to best share my knowledge with them.

To my daughter, Alexandra Voorhees, thank you for being so *forgiving* as I practiced and refined my parenting skills and for permitting me to share many of our personal and relevant experiences in this book. A third generation teacher, Alexandra readily invited me into her Universal Pre-Kindergarten class so I could experience the joy of book reading with her beautiful four-year-old children. The natural and individualized literate environment she creates with her youngters as they develop a literacy habit of mind strengthens my desire to ensure all early childhood teachers and parents have sound pedagogical literacy practices.

Thank you to my Dowling College graduate students; they remind me that we are all teacher-learners. The experiences and comments they share in my courses each semester continue to develop *my* understanding as a literacy educator and influenced many ideas for this book.

Thank you to my family for their continuous support and ensuring that I remain authentic and true to myself. Additionally, thank you to Bruce McLaughlin, for his steadfast support. From the first day I informed him that I was writing this book, his enthusiasm was heartfelt.

I am also indebted to the following people for their contributions:

To Mary Bettenhauser, Kayla Bettenhauser, Karen Cirincione, Michael Vellecca, and Douglas Whitlock—for the feedback provided at various stages of my manuscript.

To Linda Bausch, *Literacy Education Professor*; Mary Bettenhauser, *Preschool Teacher*; Karen Cirincione, *Retired Literacy Education Professor*; and Alexandra Voorhees, *Literacy Specialist and Universal Pre-Kindergarten Teacher*—for contributing to the booklist located in Appendix B.

To Zith Cavooris—for illustrating *A Wondrous World in My Head.* His talents bring my words alive each time this book is read to children.

To my young reader Harrison—for demonstrating that if children are given effective literacy environments, they naturally become lovers of books as they grow into competent literate beings.

Introduction

An Introduction to a Workshop:
It's the Parents Who Make the Difference!

Take a moment and think about your favorite song. (Mine is "Where the Boat Leaves From.") If you stop for a second and think about this tune, you can probably hear it playing over and over in your head. While the favorite song you selected probably differs from many others (as well as mine unless you are a Zac Brown fan), there are some common behaviors that we tend to engage in when developing a relationship with these tunes.

Think about what we tend to do: When a song catches our attention, we listen to it over and over again, we get to know the rhythm and words, we learn when to pause and when to stress certain parts, and we construct our own meaning from it as we make very personal connections to the song with our own lives. This is very similar to how children learn to read. You may still remember one of your favorite children's books, or your child may ask you to read his or her favorite over and over.

A long time ago, in 1908, Edmund Burke Huey, an educational psychologist, had it right when he wrote, "It all begins with parents reading to children" (103). Huey's assertion about parents can easily be supported by observing parents during shared book reading. Case in point:

In one of my past studies, mothers and their three- and four-year-old children were observed during shared book reading as a way of learning about how parents can affect young children's emergent reading development. Fathers were not purposely left out; it just happened to be that the parents who primarily read to the children in this study were mothers. The focus was on the unique nature of the individual shared book reading with mother-child pairs and how this activity influenced the children's reading behaviors when they attempted to read independently, or what is more commonly known as *pretend reading*. It is very likely that you have already seen your children make believe that they are reading.

During these shared book reading sessions, mothers were observed engaging in both meaning and print-like responses and comments when reading to their children, but some mothers did this more effectively than others. Also, these mothers appeared to have a conditioning effect on the way their children perceived reading, how their children viewed themselves as readers, and how their children approached their pretend readings of their favorite books. The mothers' attitudes and behaviors toward reading were contagious!

Specifically, the atmosphere created by the mother, the mother's understanding of how we learn to read, and the specific type of read-aloud behaviors the mother engaged in as she interacted with her child impacted the child's independent pretend readings. The young children were very sensitive to the nuances that occurred during shared book reading with their mothers, and their pretend readings reflected this.

For example, when a mother created an environment where shared book reading was a pleasurable, daily routine that encouraged her child to engage and to freely explore the book, the child was inclined to be a risk taker who confidently attempted to read independently on a daily basis. But, when a mother created an environment where the shared book reading was an effortful and unenjoyable daily routine that discouraged self-exploration, the child engaged in fewer pretend readings. Additionally, when mothers consistently brought their children's attention to the meaning of the book through questions and statements, whether it was labeling illustrations or asking what was going to happen next in the story, their children also engaged in these same types of meaning behaviors when they were pretend reading.

All so very interesting, but why is this so important? Here is why: While most new parents find pretend readings of their children's favorite books cute to watch and videotape, few realize that those pretend reading behaviors are actually critical to the literacy development of their children as they move toward conventional reading. A trained eye can actually observe children during pretend readings and identify developmental reading patterns.

In 1985, one educational researcher, Elizabeth Sulzby, created a storybook reading developmental chart to use as a tool to track young children's emerging reading behaviors. This chart can be viewed on a scale that begins when children are making picture-like attempts to read, like labeling and commenting on the illustrations but no story is formed, to print-like attempts, where children are using some aspects of the print that sound like a story, until they can read independently. Therefore, when parents read to their children, it is important to use reading behaviors that closely match those effective reading behaviors their children will need in order to read successfully.

Like learning a favorite song, children learn to read by hearing their favorite books read to them over and over again. Children listen to the book-reading voice of their parents, including intonation and pauses. They focus on those illustrations and words that delight them and that are stressed by their parents, and they ask their parents to read the book again and again. Sometimes a book is read so often that the child memorizes it, and these pretend readings sound more and more like the actual book. Some children learn to recite the book verbatim.

As children develop these behaviors, they will then become interested in figuring out which words on the page match the oral words they are reciting.

They may even ask their parents to start pointing to those words when they read them. Parents will hear their children's pretend readings move closer and closer to real (conventional) reading until their children finally match voice to print. Here is when children can point to each word as they are reading it out loud. This is when children transition from pretend reading to *real*, independent reading. This is the goal for all parents!

This book is structured with two major sections: Part I will provide the necessary background information about language and literacy learning and how one reads. Within this section, oral language development, learning theory, and the reading process will be explained. Part II describes how parents can engage in effective shared book reading with their children, which is all about application. Topics emphasized include how to create a favorable, literacy environment as well as how to make sound instructional decisions before, during, and after shared book reading. Part II will also use an accompanying children's book, *A Wondrous World in My Head* (Voorhees 2013) to demonstrate specific behaviors in which parents can engage. (See Appendix A to view this children's book.) The children's book can be fully downloaded in color online (Amazon.com/Kindle).

Each chapter of this book ends with a *Let's Review* section, which points out those most salient points presented in that chapter. Additionally, short personal stories are used throughout the book to introduce new concepts and facilitate understanding.

Furthermore, a *Final Thoughts* chapter is provided at the end of the book. A set of criteria when selecting a preschool is first offered to parents. This is followed by a touch of educational policy so parents understand what their children will be expected to achieve in kindergarten and beyond. Last, the critical role of parents in their children's early literacy development is restated, and parents are once again encouraged to nourish their children as they grow and develop into meaning-making literate beings.

Part One

BUILDING PARENTS' KNOWLEDGE ABOUT LANGUAGE, LEARNING, AND READING

Chapter One

Children Learning Their First Words Is NOT Magic

Do your children understand you when you speak to them? Are they learning to say new words every day? Learning oral language seems to happen magically without any formal instruction at all. Amazing, right? Language acquisition is a phenomenon. One only has to record daily parent-baby interactions to see how language naturally develops within meaningful contexts. Case in point:

One of the first words baby Alexandra produced was "bottle." When Alexandra was born, she wasn't very large at 6 pounds 7 ounces, but she was STARVING! Very quickly, she seemed to be twice her size, and she LOVED her bottles. It is no wonder one of her first meaningful words was "bottle."

Alexandra screamed a very angry cry when she was hungry (you remember the drill when your child cried at 2 AM or maybe you are doing it now). In order to figure out what she was crying about, that is, what she wanted to communicate, it took some trial and error. Sometimes she was tired or uncomfortable or hungry, so different ways of soothing her were tried. Asking Alexandra "Are you tired?" and rocking her, or "Do you need your diaper changed?" and changing it, or "Do you want a bottle?" and putting a bottle to her lips were routinely attempted each time Alexandra fussed.

Soon it became clear which cries communicated which needs, and so every time she seemed to cry out of hunger, Alexandra would experience a similar routine: A bottle was prepared for her and in a high-pitched voice she would hear, "Bottle, do you want a bottle?" and the bottle would be placed near her lips. One day, she produced what appeared to be a meaningful utterance when a bottle was being prepared for her because she reached out for it and uttered "baba." With pure excitement, she immediately received a response of "Bottle, do you want a bottle?"

This turn-taking conversation didn't end with this one interaction. Instead, it became a routine that occurred several times a day when her bottle was being prepared, and each time she repeated "baba," a bottle was handed to her with a big smile and enthusiastic response of "Here is your bottle!" No negative feedback was given, like "No, not baba, it is B-O-T-T-L-E." Instead her language approximation of "baba" was not only accepted but praised. It is difficult to determine how many attempts Alexandra may have made in trying out her speech of "baba" before it actually meant bottle to her, but at some point Alexandra started testing out her babbling sound of "baba" and made the connection to receiving a drink based on positive feedback.

This is just one isolated example that demonstrates how children construct meaning within a natural, everyday social context. But babies are doing this all the time within these natural contexts that are purposeful to them.

A QUICK LESSON IN LANGUAGE ACQUISITION

The fact is, humans are amazing, natural language beings; we are born with all the equipment necessary, like our vocal chords and our brains, which are wired to understand and produce language. The renowned linguist Noam Chomsky (1968) contended that since everyone learned language, it must be something we are born with; he referred to the child as a "Language Acquisition Device." What does he mean by this? Humans have all the mechanisms necessary to understand and produce language.

Imitation plays a role in learning language. According to the theories of B. F. Skinner (1957), children mimic parents' speech, and they are often given reinforcement for doing this. Most parents can surely recall a word or phrase their child mimicked after listening to them or another member of their family. Sometimes they are words parents would rather they not repeat!

Very young children, however, also produce their own *unique utterances* that they have never heard before, and these constructions are based on the meanings of things. For example, "I'm drinky" rather than "I'm thirsty" was a unique utterance Alexandra made as a toddler. She had certainly never heard this utterance spoken before. Unique utterances, however, are strongly supported by Lois Bloom's research written in 1970 demonstrating that children talk about the meanings of what they already experience prior to and as they develop and try out rules for their language. The utterance of "I'm drinky" surely demonstrates her connection of meaning with her acquiring knowledge of grammar rules.

And finally, according to two distinguished educational and cognitive psychologists, Jerome Bruner (1977) and Lev Vygotsky (1986), in order for children's language to develop, they must also be in situations where they will practice communication by talking to other humans. It is through *social interaction* that children test out their hypotheses about language within purposeful contexts with another more capable language user, like a parent, to support their attempts.

Two researchers, Hart and Risley (1995), conducted extensive research on oral language development and found that children's learning depended on how much exposure and involvement they had in the language events. One study found that in one hour some parents say fewer than five hundred words, while other parents state over three thousand words! In short, the amount of blended parent talk with child practice talk was essential to language achievement.

Young children learn a lot of words, and quickly. In 2001, Louisa Moats researched this and estimated that by the time children enter first grade, they know between five thousand and twenty thousand words. This number varies considerably, depending on the number of language experiences the child has been exposed to and the type and effectiveness of these language interactions. So parents are VERY important!

SETTING UP SUCCESS FOR LEARNING

There are many environmental factors that contribute to the acquisition of language and literacy. In 1988, Brian Cambourne, a literacy education professor from Australia, developed seven conditions he believed were crucial to learning, which many teachers follow today. They are:

1. *Immersion*: Children need to be embedded in meaningful texts (both oral and written) of all kinds.
2. *Demonstration*: Children need good modeling where they are shown how these texts are understood and used.
3. *Expectation*: Children need to feel as though those around them believe they will succeed because they have been placed in contexts where they will be successful.
4. *Responsibility*: Children need to be empowered by making their own decisions about their learning.
5. *Use*: Children need many opportunities to employ and practice what they are learning.
6. *Approximation:* Children need to know that it is okay to make mistakes as they practice the *bits* of knowledge they are developing.
7. *Response*: Children need to see and hear relative, appropriate, and timely feedback from their supporters (in this case, parents).

Additionally, learning will come to a screeching halt if during *Immersion* and *Demonstration* children are not *engaged* in the process. Children need to be involved and part of the process from the very beginning, rather than passive observers. As Cambourne (1988) stated many times, this will only occur when the literacy tasks are perceived as doable, purposeful, risk-free, and with no unpleasant consequences if the child fails. Otherwise learners are often unsuccessful.

These learning components are not isolated for only acquiring early literacy skills. Case in point:

At eleven years old, I was forced to be in a piano concert by my teacher and parents. The piano teacher picked a classical piece (Mozart) with no regard to my interests or ability. It was an intimidating piece from the start and memorizing it became a daunting task. No one was permitted to use the sheet music during the concert as a safety net. Yikes!

You probably can predict what happened at the concert. It was a disaster. Sweaty hands, fumbling fingers, missed bar lines, and finally running off stage was the lived-through experience. Why? One, there was no motivation to practice a musical piece that was not personally selected—it lacked purpose; two, the idea of playing in front of a large group was disconcerting to say the least—it was risky; and three, the music composition was just too difficult and all confidence was lost—it wasn't doable. This can also be related to one's self-efficacy. (For Your Information: Self-efficacy is the belief one has about his or her ability to learn and carry out a specific task or behavior [Bandura 1997].)

The learning conditions this music teacher set up had "disaster" written all over it. Unfortunately, there is always a victim in these circumstances. Embarrassment, humiliation, and failure were learned; this is not what teachers (or parents) want to achieve. Sometimes these experiences, where critical learning conditions are missing, have such a damaging impact on future learning that it affects us for a lifetime. Had the teacher allowed for self-selection based on ability level (perhaps a ragtime song like "Maple Leaf Rag," which was a favorite and still easily played from memory forty-one years later), there would have been a very different, and much more positive, outcome. Success increases self-efficacy and also fosters more frequent practicing.

Revisiting the ideas of Bruner (1977) and Vygotsky (1986) about the social nature of language acquisition and development, we see that children learn to understand and produce language through social interaction with proficient language users, and these proficient language users are often their parents. Naturally, parents create developmentally appropriate contexts.

First, parents, as the language experts, model the use of language. Second, parents are tuned into their child's current language abilities and therefore create language activities that are based on their understanding of their child and are not too difficult or too easy for their child. Third, parents assist (often called *scaffolding*) their child's language attempts, by acting as mediators or supports as they guide their child to succeed. And fourth, parents raise their expectations and the difficulty of the language activities as the child develops. This is good teaching; effective teachers instruct this way all the time in the classroom.

This follows a learning model developed by educators/researchers Pearson and Gallagher (1983), called the *Gradual Release of Responsibility* model. Parents (as do teachers) actually engage their children in explicit and implicit instruction. First, they demonstrate how to communicate, then they actively engage their children in the communication process but with parents' help (which is called *guided practice*), and finally, they gradually release the communication task onto their children until their children can do it independently. So basically, the responsibility of communication changes from the parents to the children as children develop their oral language. Please see figure 1.1, which demonstrates this process.

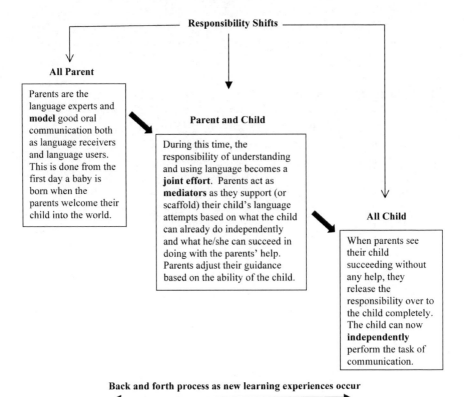

Figure 1.1.   Gradual Release of Responsibility from Parent to Child
(Source: Model of explicit instruction adapted from Pearson and Gallagher 1983)

LET'S REVIEW

The ideas in this chapter are complex and warrant a quick review. The chapter began with a personal story that explained how Alexandra learned her first word, "bottle." This language event included all seven of Cambourne's (1988) learning conditions, which can easily be identified.

- First, Alexandra was **immersed** in a context that was very meaningful and purposeful to her, and to every baby. Babies are hungry and they want to be fed.
- Second, because at first Alexandra could not convey exactly what she wanted, oral communication was **demonstrated** by asking her questions and then placing Alexandra within the appropriate context. Clearly, most of the responsibility rested on the parent at this time (for example, "Are you tired?" as she was rocked or "Are you hungry?" and then placing the bottle near her lips).
- Third, Alexandra was never treated as though she would not learn to understand and speak. She was **expected** to learn the English language and to engage in these turn-taking communication routines as naturally as when older, more competent, family members talk to one another.
- Fourth, by placing Alexandra in different contexts, like asking her if she was tired and rocking her, or asking if she was hungry and giving her a bottle, some **responsibility** was beginning to be placed onto her. If Alexandra did not want the bottle, she eventually would spit it out or push it away. If she was not tired, she would keep crying when she was placed in her crib, or when she was more mobile, she would squirm and try to get out. Undeniably, this is a form of answering/responding. As she developed, Alexandra became more responsible for her own communication as she began to practice oral sounds and say meaningful words.
- Fifth, these communication routines were ongoing throughout the day. Alexandra had many opportunities to **use** or try out what she was beginning to learn about language.
- Sixth, when Alexandra said "baba," and for the first time it was interpreted as the word "bottle," her effort was praised. The oral language **approximations** were not reprimanded but instead accepted.
- Seventh, not only was Alexandra's utterance of "baba" accepted, but also positive **feedback** for her attempt was provided by responses of pure joy, as well as by her being satisfied with her bottle.

If this communication event had been meaningless and/or too difficult for Alexandra, then this learning cycle would not have taken place. However, authentic situations were created that were *just right* for Alexandra so that she could begin learning the meaning and production of single words.

Do parents always provide *perfect learning environments*? Of course not. But when parents are active, reflective observers of their children's abilities, they pick up on when they have created a situation that is either too difficult or too easy, and they adjust the task accordingly. Parents often naturally know how to develop their children's oral language and how to create appropriate learning environments. As you go about your everyday lives, see if you can catch yourself or another parent of a young child engaging in these essential conditions of learning. You will be amazed at how often parents do this.

Chapter Two

Teaching Children to Read Is as Natural as Learning to Ride a Bike

When we are learning something new, it is probably easiest for us to break down the task into smaller parts, learn those smaller parts, and then put them all together. This is commonsense instruction, right? Well, perhaps not always. Case in point:

Alexandra couldn't wait to try out her new, shiny, pink bicycle when she turned five. She was so excited, and her mother was eager to teach her. So, to simplify the task of learning to ride, there were three readiness skills she needed to learn: 1) pedaling, 2) steering, and 3) balance. Instead of trying out her bicycle from the day it was brought home from the store, a little classroom with a blackboard, children's chair, and stationary bike was set up in the basement. Thinking that pedaling should be learned before the other two skills, a diagram of the pedals with gears was drawn on the blackboard so that she could learn about the pedaling motion of pushing down and how the peddle rotates in a clockwise motion.

Although Alexandra didn't seem too interested, she was told this would help her when she was actually riding her bicycle. So she listened. Then, she practiced pedaling on the stationary bike. She was great; she barely needed any practice.

The next day, the second skill was introduced to her, which was steering. Following the same instructional format, a diagram of steering was placed on the blackboard, and the term was defined as moving the handlebars from left to right and right to left in the direction you want to go. Alexandra then practiced moving the loosened handle bar on the stationary bike from left to right, right to left, and holding it straight ahead. Alexandra had some difficulty with this skill. Her steering motions were jerky, and she was confused as to which side was left and which side was right. But she finally did get it, and at that point she asked could she PLEASE try out her new, shiny, pink bicycle, but she was told there was more to learn first. Alexandra made a face and stomped up the stairs, but instructing her correctly would be well worth it.

The following day, Alexandra barely spoke as she practiced her final skill, balance. One last time, a diagram was drawn, and the term was discussed. Alexandra then performed the task of sitting on the bike and trying to keep her balance as long as she could without tipping over. Surprisingly, this was the easiest task for her. It had now been almost a week since we bought the new, shiny, pink bicycle so she didn't really respond to any positive feedback given to her.

Finally, she accomplished all three skills. She was ready, and up the stairs and out the door she went in a flash. Alexandra sat on her new, shiny, pink bicycle with a huge smile on her face. Holding the bicycle for a second or two while she sat on the seat, Alexandra started pedaling as hard as any five-year-old could, but she fell to the ground. Still very determined, Alexandra hopped right back on her bike; she was reminded not to forget balance and steering straight. Alexandra made her second attempt, but a few feet later, she was down on the ground once more.

She attempted this about three more times, but to no avail. This day ended with a lot of tears and scrapes both on her and her new, shiny, pink bicycle. The next morning, Alexandra refused to try riding again. That weekend, her dad told Alexandra that this time he would hold onto the back of her bike and run with her as she rode until he knew she could do it on her own just like his dad had done when he learned to ride a bike.

Little by little, he started letting go sooner and sooner. As she practiced all morning, her dad noticed Alexandra was jerking the handle bars and leaning too far when she was turning, so he showed her how to keep her posture when she was turning. This worked and, although she fell a few times, the fact that she could feel herself riding motivated her to hop right back on the bike, until she was riding down the street by the afternoon. Success had been achieved.

The question that needs to be answered is, "Why was Alexandra's dad so much more successful than her mom?"

INVITING CHILDREN TO BE MEMBERS
OF THE LITERACY CLUB

Before reading this next section, take a few moments to answer the following questions about learning to read:

1. How did you learn to read?

_____

_____

_____

_____

_____

2. Do you believe you can influence your child's reading development before he or she enters formal schooling (kindergarten)? If so, how?

   _____

   _____

   _____

   _____

   _____

3. Do you think children can learn to read before formal schooling? Why or
   why not?

   _____

   _____

   _____

   _____

   _____

4. What skills, if any, do you think your child needs to know before he or
   she begins to read?

   _____

   _____

   _____

   _____

   _____

5. Does your child exhibit any behaviors that you would classify as reading
   or reading-like behaviors? If yes, can you give examples?

   _____

   _____

   _____

   _____

   _____

6. If your child is attending kindergarten, do you believe you have prepared
   your child for academic reading success?

   _____

   _____

   _____

   _____

   _____

There are two major perspectives in regard to how children learn to read:
reading readiness and *emergent literacy*. Reading readiness follows a part-
to-whole approach when teaching children to read. It is a more traditional

belief that children must master specific basic skills in a certain order before we can even think of teaching them to read and placing a book in their hands to read independently. This perspective of learning literacy also includes the assumption that reading is difficult and unnatural to learn (different from the natural process of learning oral language) and that children have little knowledge about reading until after they are provided formal teaching (usually this begins in kindergarten). This perspective has been challenged over the past two decades; however, it still exists in many educational settings.

Today, many would agree that literacy learning is taking place in the home at a very young age. Children are in the process of becoming literate from the day they are born. Similar to the acquisition of spoken language, children's reading abilities develop in real-life settings while they are engaged in real-life activities. The term *emergent literacy* is used to describe these early reading behaviors that will eventually develop into conventional reading (Sulzby and Teale 1995).

According to this perspective, from the very beginning (birth), children are naturally becoming literate and learning about written language before entering school. So, more specifically, children who are read to often at home actively figure out how language in books is different from oral language. For example, when reading "Once upon a time there were three little pigs," this storybook language sounds different from the language we use in oral conversation. Children learn this difference when their parents read to them frequently, model reading behaviors, and discuss the story. A parent may also direct the child to the illustrations of a picture book, demonstrating to the child that picture cues will tell the story and represent the words that are being read.

Children, if given the opportunity, will internalize many reading behaviors. As stated in the Introduction, by putting favorite books that have been read over and over to children in their hands, we can see that they have a great deal of knowledge about books and are becoming literate, *meaning-making* beings. Their knowledge about books may include book handling behaviors (like understanding that the cover of a book has a title, holding the book correctly, opening to the first page of text, and looking at and turning pages from left to right) and pretend reading behaviors (like labeling pictures, identifying print features, and reading with story-like characteristics).

The act of reading aloud is one way parents welcome their children into what Frank Smith (2004) termed "the literacy club." This is a socially created activity in which language interactions of the parent and child accompany the book reading. Research shows that during shared book reading, parents and their children are actively constructing meaning when they discuss the story. Both parent and child are partners as the parent guides the child through questioning and statement behaviors.

Some shared book reading styles of parents, however, foster children's attainment of literacy better than others. Effective dialoging (that is, involving children in the reading experience in a conversation-like manner) of content and text components provides children with more opportunities to participate and to think about and synthesize ideas. As with oral language development, parents notice and support their children's growing competence and vary the learning strategies within their shared book reading rituals. As the child's literacy competence develops, parents gradually give more responsibility to the child, until, ultimately, the child adopts the necessary skills and strategies and conducts the reading task independently.

Independent reading attempts are part of the process of learning to read. When a child pretend reads, he or she is practicing those behaviors learned from parent behaviors during the shared book reading. Children's independent functioning with books is often called *emergent storybook reading* or *reenactments* and is defined as occasions when children *read* or *reenact* familiar books in ways that are not yet conventional reading but which can be characterized by acts of reading (Sulzby and Teale 1991). This "reading" sounds very different from their conversation surrounding the text. Instead they *sound* like they are reading and act like they are reading as they turn the pages, demonstrating their growing awareness of features of written language. This pretend reading process is eventually fine-tuned and develops into conventional reading.

LET'S REVIEW

To clear up any confusion, let us connect the reading readiness and emergent literacy perspectives with the example of how Alexandra learned to ride a bicycle. By breaking the task of riding a bike into specific skills that need to be mastered one at a time which then build on the next skill, a part-to-whole approach was followed. It seems to make perfect sense to break down a task to smaller, easier pieces; however, there were several problems with this approach, and clearly, it was not effective.

- First, an incorrect assumption was made that Alexandra had developed no knowledge and skills prior to her bicycle lessons, but of course she had. Alexandra may not have been able to describe steering or pedaling or balance, but each day, by her interacting with her world, these skills were *emerging* at least to some degree. By forcing her to work on some skills that she had already mastered, she was not only bored, but frustrated.
- Second, an *order* of skill difficulty was developed, and a new skill was not introduced until the easier skill was mastered. However, this was just

an arbitrary decision. Since all children are *unique beings* based on past experiences and their own makeup, another child may have mastered a different skill first.

- Third, each skill was isolated from the next skill. Alexandra was asked to engage in the very *unnatural process* of working on just one small part of bike riding at a time. In order to ride a bicycle, our bodies *orchestrate* many skills at one time. Alexandra was not given any experiences to do this. For Alexandra to learn how to ride her bike, she needed to get on the bicycle and *practice* riding it. This is probably how most of us learned how to ride a bike, as well as drive a car: not by way of abstract instruction, but rather by doing it firsthand.

This was evidently a *bicycle riding readiness* perspective. So, long before Alexandra got on that bicycle, her bicycle skills were emerging through everyday experiences as both her brain and body developed. An observant mother (and teacher) would have realized that Alexandra had already acquired some of these skills, and now she needed the appropriate explicit instruction and experiences that would guide her to ride her bicycle independently.

Alexandra's dad followed an *emergent bicycle riding* perspective, which proved to be much more effective. When Alexandra was on her bike, her dad observed what she was doing well and where she would need guidance. He realized that she was having difficulty with shifting her body to one side when she turned, which was causing her to fall, so he explicitly demonstrated this for her, showing her how to be sure she remained centered on the seat. Then she tried to do this again while riding. He provided scaffolding based on Alexandra's ability level. Alexandra's dad followed a whole-to-part (based on the child's needs) to whole perspective.

Now take a moment and reread your answers to those questions at the beginning of this chapter. What do your answers say about your beliefs in regard to how children learn to read and the influence you have on your child's reading development? Your behaviors, goals, and how you respond to your child's reactions and initiations during shared book reading strongly reflect these beliefs.

If you identified yourself as having a more traditional type of belief system for literacy learning (reading readiness), then don't feel bad. Most parents hold belief systems that are based on their own instructional history, that is, how they were taught at home and in school. But perhaps you are beginning to shift your thinking toward the idea that children are emerging literate beings from the day they are born. The next step is to learn about what good (proficient) readers do when they read. *Did you ever think about what you do when you are engaging in the act of reading?*

Chapter Three

Can Our Brains Really Attend to Two Tasks at the Same Time?

Multitasking—the ability to perform two or more tasks at the same time. People state that they successfully do this every day. Can our brains, however, actually think about and act on two tasks simultaneously? Not really, or at least there are limitations in one's ability to multitask. Case in point:

Teaching Alexandra, at seventeen, to drive was an adventure. One day, she asked to practice on the way to an uncle's house, but soon after getting into the car, Alexandra started to explain that she would be late that night because she was going to a party. This didn't go over too well, so what started out to be very light conversation for this short journey ended up becoming an argument.

Alexandra, determined to attend this party, debated like an experienced attorney as the conversation intensified. She was given every parental reason why she wasn't attending this party, and as the argument hit a climax, she was turning into her uncle's driveway, which had a brick pillar on each side, and as you might have guessed, "BAM" she hit the pillar on the right side! Luckily, no one was hurt (just the car), but it is certainly a lesson in how the brain functions, the limitations of the brain, and how good readers read.

WHY CAN WE WALK, TALK, AND CHEW GUM AT THE SAME TIME?

This question can be answered by connecting the process of reading to the *driving the car* scenario and will help you to understand how the brain works. Readers engage in two major components (see figure 3.1).

As soon as readers begin any reading task, they activate their background knowledge about the content of the story or topic and begin to connect it to

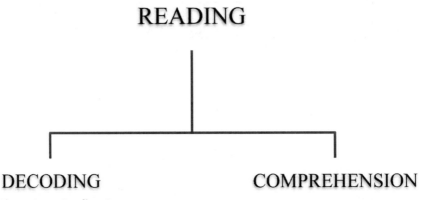

Figure 3.1.   Reading Components

the text as they begin reading. One must be able to decode the text, that is, identify the words, and construct meaning (while decoding), which is comprehension. Each of these processes occurs together, not in a linear fashion.

There is a little catch, though, that involves the limitations of the brain. The brain can only attend to one task at a time. You might be saying to yourself that this doesn't make sense because all people engage in more than one task at a time. For example, you can walk, talk, and chew gum all at the same time. So can all people, or most. You can also drive and have a conversation with passengers at the same time. This is because when you engage in more than one task simultaneously, some of the tasks are automatic. The term *automatic* means that these tasks are instantaneous and completed without conscious attention.

Experienced drivers can drive automatically because they have many years of practice; they can easily engage in an extensive conversation while driving. Their brains are attending more to the conversation (must give conscious thought to this) than to the driving, which is mostly automatic. You probably have had the experience of driving to the same destination for the millionth time and became absorbed in your inner thoughts rather than the driving. Before you knew it, there you were at your desired location. You wondered, "How did I get here?" The answer is quite simple; your ability to drive to that same location day after day became automatic; no conscious effort had to be given to the task.

Relating this back to reading, as stated previously, readers must engage in decoding (identifying the print) and comprehension (understanding) when they read. More specifically, decoding must be somewhat automatic if readers are going to engage in active comprehension. Comprehension can never be automatic because readers are always actively trying to figure out what the author's intentions are as they are reading.

Readers are constructing meaning, which is not an automatic task. So as proficient readers, you decode text automatically and construct meaning simultaneously; you can easily do this because your brains have the ability to *attention switch* between decoding the text (relatively effortlessly) and comprehension (which is an active process). Comprehension supports decoding and decoding supports comprehension.

What is attention switching? Here is an example. Have you ever been to a party and someone started a conversation with you that was not very interesting or deep, and the person was providing you with every single unimportant detail of the event being explained, so you started listening to another couple's conversation close by that seemed much more interesting? You were still listening enough to Vivian Verbatim in front of you, and responding with "Ah ha" "Um-humm" and "Really?" as you looked at Vivian, but you were also able to focus on the more interesting conversation that was near you. You are basically just switching attention back and forth between the two conversations. This has been referred to as the *cocktail party phenomenon* (Rosenblatt 1994).

However, there is a reciprocal relationship between any two tasks in which the brain engages. Humans can switch back and forth between the two tasks as long as at least one task is requiring little attention (like the "Vivian" conversation). People do it all the time very successfully, but if the brain starts to focus too much on one of the two tasks, then the brain will not have enough attention available (often called *cognitive capacity*) to attend to the second task, and then the brain is unsuccessful with at least one of the two tasks. This is when you get *caught* by Vivian Verbatim!

Revisiting Alexandra's driving session scenario, you probably now realize why she was not successful (and why we can *multitask* with some activities, but not with others). Alexandra was attempting to attention switch between engaging in driving and the argument. She failed to attention switch between driving and debating as the argument intensified because neither was automatic to her and both required a great deal of her cognitive energy. What occurred can be referred to as a *trade-off of attention* (LaBerge and Samuels 1974). Because Alexandra was giving too much attention/mental energy to the argument, there was not enough attention/mental energy left to be directed toward the driving. Hence, there was a breakdown in her driving.

The same principle follows for readers and for drivers. If a reader gives too much attention to decoding the text because much of the decoding is not automatic, then he or she will not get much out of the actual reading. In other words, this is when there is a breakdown in comprehension. Clearly, decoding automatically is critical to proficient reading as much as driving automatically is critical to the driver.

So how do readers become automatic at decoding? They practice reading texts over and over; in short, becoming an adequate driver requires a lot of time behind the wheel, and in order to become an adequate decoder, readers must spend a great deal of time in front of books practicing the decoding of text. Through practice, practice, practice, readers accumulate more and more information in their brains related to the task, and this allows them to become experts in that area.

INTERACTIONS WITH OUR ENVIRONMENT ARE SIMILAR TO THE INTERACTIONS BETWEEN READER AND TEXT

Reading is a complex process, so besides the importance of decoding automatically, there are other important issues to discuss. A very important component when reading is the readers' background knowledge, that is, every single experience they have accumulated up until the point of the current reading. This is similar to your understanding of any interaction you have in your environment. Case in point:

Did you ever watch a child the first time he or she sees and pets a dog? There is often pure delight in the feel of the dog's fur, the lick of the dog's tongue, and the friendliness of the dog's demeanor. Then the first time a dog barks, it startles the child, but as the dog barks and licks the child's face and wags its tail, the child understands that barking dogs are friendly. These interactions teach children a great deal about dogs. They learn about the features of a dog and how they act and sound. Each time children interact with different dogs and have similar experiences, their knowledge about dogs grows stronger and deeper. They believe all dogs are friendly.

When Alexandra was about two-and-a-half years old, her dad thought it would be a good idea to adopt a rather large seven-month-old brown Labrador as the family pet. Alexandra, having had many friendly experiences by now with dogs in her young life, expected the dog to act similarly to dogs in those past experiences. But as it turns out, this brown Labrador was rather aggressive, and soon after he was introduced to Alexandra, he began to relentlessly chew on her hands and feet and knock her over. Clearly, Alexandra's prior experiences did not prepare her for this new experience.

This transaction with the aggressive Labrador was unexpected, and therefore, it confused Alexandra. This is because she had never had any prior experiences with unfriendly dogs. She had learned that dogs come in all sizes and colors and shapes. This all made sense to her. Yet, based on her past experiences with dogs, she predicted that all dogs were friendly, which is not reality. However, it didn't take Alexandra too many experiences with this brown Labrador to alter her thinking about dogs, that is, that some dogs are gentle, and others are not. Alexandra spent the next two days begging to be held until her dad finally realized the dog needed to go!

The above dog scenario is a good example of how Piaget (1957) explains cognitive development. Sometimes children *assimilate* incoming information to fit into their existing ideas. However, other times, their existing understanding (in this case the aggressive dog) does not work, that is, it does not make sense with what they already know about something, and if this happens, they change their thinking in order to deal with and understand the new situation.

Your understanding of anything, including your understanding of what you read, is based on the simple premise that you are always predicting in order to understand, and your predictions are based on your past experiences or background knowledge (Smith 2004). Additionally, you do not need to take in every single bit of new information because you can make predictions based on past experiences. But now, think about whenever you have been confused before. It is usually because someone acted in a different way from what you were used to, or you had never heard of something before, or in short, you had never previously experienced anything like it.

Try experiencing this when you read. Read the following sentences about jumping rope from an article in *Self* magazine:

> Jumping rope is the calorie zapper you shouldn't skip: it incinerates 100 big ones in fewer than 8 minutes. . . . Hold your elbows at sides, bent 90 degrees, with arms slightly forward, palms up. For smooth turns, it's all in the wrists. Rotate hands, not the entire arm, in small circles. Contracting shoulders, triceps and biceps throughout will help you control your revolutions and sculpt arms. (Emerick 2012, 72)

Now try reading the next few sentences from *Modern Physics from a to Z^0* describing the Schroedinger Wave Equation:

> In the particle in the box, the wave function is precisely equal to zero at the boundaries of the box. In the finite square-well with the large value of V(0), the wave function will be very small at the boundaries, but not identically zero. Since the integral of the square of the wave function from $-$infinity to $+$infinity is unity the wave function . . . must go to zero at x = $-$infinity and x = $+$infinity. Therefore, the wave function is identically zero at x = $-$infinity and x = $+$infinity. The solutions to the finite square-well wave functions look similar to the particle in the box solutions, except that the wave functions will have a small extension beyond the well boundaries. (Rohlf 1994, 200–201)

Had enough of this reading? Did you make sense of it? Would you be able to explain what this passage was about as easily as you would be able to explain the best way to jump rope? Most of you (unless you understand quantum mechanics) were able to understand the first passage better than the second passage. The second passage was confusing. Why?

The answer has to do with an individual's background knowledge. Most people have the background knowledge/experiences to connect to the information in the first passage; many of you have jumped rope before, so you can connect your personal experiences and vocabulary with the new information in the passage. Schema (that is, a mental framework of the concept) for jumping rope is available so you are able to comprehend the passage.

Most people do not, however, have an equal amount of information available to them about physics to comprehend the second passage (unless you are a physics expert). Hence, few connections can be made. This means that, although many of you may be able to memorize some of the information in the second passage, you do not *understand* this information. You do not have experience in this area, you do not recognize the parts that were mentioned in the passage, and you cannot assign topic-specific meanings to the vocabulary used in this passage. In short, readers who do not have the schema for understanding the physics passage will incur a breakdown in comprehension.

When readers have background knowledge about what they are reading, they can activate that knowledge and connect it to the new information they are reading. When readers do not have the background knowledge about the topic being read, then the reader cannot make those new-to-known connections and must rely more on the print. If readers rely solely on the print, and make no connections to their background knowledge or what has now been introduced as schema, they do not comprehend.

Why is this so important? Because, in order to understand anything, one must be able to make predictions and confirm those predictions. Readers cannot do this if they do not have any background knowledge. So then how do readers get these experiences? How can anyone ever learn anything new if they don't have the background knowledge? One way is the same way little Alexandra learned about dogs, and that is through actual demonstration and experience. If you want to truly learn about Schroedinger Wave Equation facts (*my guess is you don't!*), then you would need someone to demonstrate some aspects of it, or perhaps make an analogy to it with something you know, in order to develop schema for it.

PREDICTION IS COMPREHENSION'S BEST FRIEND

Let us connect prediction and comprehension a little bit better. Based on your prior knowledge, you know that when you get up in the morning, there will be a floor underneath you as you hop off the bed. You understand that when you walk into the bathroom, your toothbrush will be waiting for you in the same place it was left the night before, and you know if you look out your window, you will see your car sitting in the driveway where you left it the night before. You can comprehend these basic everyday occurrences because of your past experiences. There are no surprises, you can *predict* these things based on your prior experiences, and when you feel the floor, or see your toothbrush or get in your car, you are confirming these predictions. But this is done all automatically at this point, because it has happened over and over the same way.

Can you imagine what life would be like if you could not predict based on what you learned from past experiences? For example, if each time you walked into a new bathroom, you would be in a state of wonder because you could not connect it to your background knowledge about bathrooms. But we all know that when you walk into a bathroom, there is a sink, mirror, toilet, and shower.

So as we interact with our environment, we constantly predict based on past experiences, but what happens when our predictions no longer make sense? Case in point:

One morning the car was gone from the driveway where it had been parked the night before; the prediction that the car would be there in the morning was not confirmed. Now, a new prediction must be constructed based on all prior experiences and knowledge. Maybe the car was stolen! If this is the case, then the police would need to be called, but upon entering the house to make that phone call, further information becomes available about the missing car. It is a note: "Stopped over while you were in the shower. I need to borrow your car for an hour. Sorry, I'll be back soon. Love you, Alexandra."

Now, clearly, the second prediction has again been disconfirmed as more information is gathered, so the police will not be alerted, but with this added information, the prediction-confirming thought cycle continues. A new prediction is now made—something must have happened with Alexandra's car. When Alexandra shows up a few minutes later and explains that she was dropped off because her car wouldn't start, but she needed to go to a doctor's appointment, the new prediction is confirmed and understanding takes place. (And her mother can now add this to her prior experiences about her daughter; that is, she will borrow anything without asking, even the car!)

This scenario can easily be related to the reading process. Readers always use their background knowledge when reading. They make predictions as they read, and then confirm these predictions as they receive further information. Read the following statement: *I'd like to order a pizza pie with mushrooms, extra cheese, and p_____.* Can you predict what the last word in the sentence is based on using your prior knowledge about pizza and your word knowledge about something that makes sense in the blank and begins with a *P*?

Probably *pony*, or *pumpkin*, or *participate*, or any other word that made no sense didn't come to mind. This is based on past experiences because your brain would tell you "That doesn't make any sense" as you monitor your understanding. And because you were given part of the spelling, the letter *P*, you also used your background knowledge about the spelling of words, which helped you. In addition, it is most likely that you filled in a noun, because you also have knowledge about the part of speech that would best fit in that sentence. Most predictions probably included *pepperoni* or maybe *peppers*.

Here is another example: Try to complete the following statement: *I'd like to order an Italian hero with lettuce, tomato, and o*_____. You might have read it as *olives*, because this is what you like on your sandwich, but you may have read it as *onions* (or some other word that made sense and began with *O*). Now if the next sentence in the passage was *I changed my mind; I don't want to have bad breath so forget the o*_____, then your thinking changes.

As a good reader, you are monitoring your prediction (which is a guess), and now that you read this new information, you disconfirmed your prediction of *olives* because you know from your schema (or background knowledge) about olives that they don't make your breath stink. On the other hand, if you read it as *onions*, you are monitoring your own prediction, and now that you received further information from the text, you confirmed your prediction because, in fact, onions do give you bad breath and you construct ideas the author intended.

Readers are continually using their background knowledge about meaning, language, and letters/sounds as they predict what the next word, next sentence, and next paragraph will be about, using the text as their guide. (For your information, this is sometimes described as being perceptually parsimonious, that is, using the least amount of information from different resources in order to make a decision.) If a reader's prediction is not confirmed but rather disconfirmed, then he or she goes back and reads again, or reads on and then makes new predictions. As predictions are confirmed, readers naturally continue connecting the information to the information they already constructed about the passage and continue reading.

Also, please note that readers are able to figure out the missing word based on their background knowledge, the context of the sentence, and the first letter or spelling patterns in the word. This is important because it is demonstrating that readers DO NOT have to look at every letter of every word, but in fact, just select enough information that is needed in order to make a reasonable prediction or guess. As you continued to read the sentences about the Italian hero, you sampled more text (not every letter or every word, though), which allowed your brains to confirm or disconfirm your original prediction.

LET'S REVIEW

Proficient readers

1. decode text automatically so their brains can attend to constructing the author's intended meaning (Think back to Alexandra's mini car accident and how her brain couldn't attend to both the driving and the argument.);

2. use their background knowledge about the topic (schema) and their knowledge of language in order to make predictions and construct meaning (Think back to the jumping rope text verses the Schroedinger Wave Equation facts.);

3. sample only enough of the text that they need to make a reasonable prediction (guess) because they use their background knowledge (Think back to how you were able to easily guess the word "pepperoni" using both your prior knowledge of eating pizza (your schema) and your knowledge of words that begin with P and fit your schema about pizza toppings.); and

4. confirm or disconfirm their predictions based on more information that they receive as they continue to read (Think back to your prediction about the Italian hero. If you predicted onions in the first sentence, by the second sentence you monitored your guess and confirmed it because onions give you bad breath. If you predicted another word, like olives, in the first sentence, by the second sentence, your ability to monitor your understanding told you that your guess didn't make sense, and you disconfirmed your prediction based on more information your brain selected.)

See figure 3.2 for a simple diagram displaying the orchestrated reading process of the brain during proficient reading; perhaps this will help you visualize the ideas that have been presented in this chapter.

Proficient readers are problem solvers. As soon as readers see the cover of a book, they relate the topic of the book to what they know. Readers decode the text, search for the author's intended meaning, and construct their own meaning based on what they already know. Because readers must focus on meaning, they use the text as a guide to activate (start thinking about) their background knowledge about the topic in order to make predictions and confirm or disconfirm these predictions. There is great potential for a breakdown in comprehension IF they don't have adequate background knowledge about the topic, or they don't activate that knowledge. Once predictions are confirmed, this information is connected to what they already know, and now this new information becomes part of their background information.

So here are two very important pieces of information to remember when reading to your children:

1. Providing your children with authentic real-life experiences as well as secondary experiences (like reading to them) is critical for developing their background knowledge.

2. Reading favorite storybooks over and over again so your children are repeatedly exposed to the same text is critical as they begin to make voice to print matches and develop their decoding automaticity.

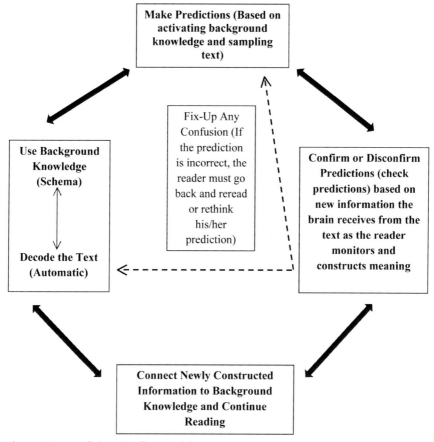

Figure 3.2. Proficient Reading Model
(Source: Model of Proficient Silent Reading adapted from Goodman and Burke 1980.)

Wow, that was a lot of information! Be assured that these two critical ideas will be demonstrated and explained throughout the remainder of the book. Part I was important because you needed to develop some background knowledge or *schema* for Part II, which is all about engaging in the shared book reading experience with your children. If you did not, you may have had a similar experience to the one you had when reading about the Schroedinger Wave Equation! Hopefully, you now have all the background information you need about language and the reading process in order to understand Part II, so let us move onward.

Part Two

PARENTS AS MEDIATORS: MAKING EFFECTIVE INSTRUCTIONAL DECISIONS

Chapter Four

If She Doesn't Like Carrots, Then Don't Keep Feeding Them to Her!

To be a proficient reader, one must practice, practice, practice! So what motivates us to actually *want* to engage in any task over and over again? What type of environment is conducive to fostering intrinsic motivation and nourishing a positive attitude? Very simply, we must like it. Case in point:

Many new parents read every parent magazine possible for advice on all sorts of issues; nutrition is often at the top of the list. Alexandra's mother once read about the importance of young children eating carrots. So as you might have guessed, the cabinet was quickly filled with carrot baby food. (Carrots are her mother's favorite!) Alexandra loved vegetables mixed with pastina, but surprisingly, the first day she tried this mixture, Alexandra shut her mouth tight, turned her head, pushed the spoon away with her hand, and refused to eat it.

So the next day, Alexandra was given carrots again . . . and again . . . and again. She became more and more determined not to eat those carrots, but CARROTS ARE GOOD FOR YOU! Each day, carrot puree would land all over Alexandra's hands, highchair. and mouth; they were delicious, but not to her. This routine would always end with crying; it was an endless struggle, mother against daughter.

Finally after about a week of these to-dos, Alexandra's grandmother, watching from the sidelines, turned and said, "Sweetheart, if Alexandra doesn't like carrots, perhaps you should stop feeding them to her." Then she added, "She seems to like sweet potatoes a lot so probably eating this vegetable is as healthy as the carrots. Since you like the carrots, maybe you should continue to eat them." And then she just smiled, but not without concluding, "You are creating what seems to be a stressful and unenjoyable eating routine by forcing this food on her."

Such simple thoughts. Alexandra was an individual, with individual ideas, likes, and dislikes, even at the age of one, and although probably most parents secretly hope their children will have the same ideas as they do, good parenting means fostering their individualism and free thought, not controlling it. Some people like carrots and hate lima beans, and serving lima beans each day for lunch, no matter how good they are for you, is not going to change this.

So what is the lesson learned from this story, and how does it relate to good parenting and reading?

NURTURING LITERACY ENGAGEMENT

Early literacy engagement has a great deal to do with first facilitating children's positive attitudes toward reading. This occurs based on the environment parents create during the home literacy practice of shared book reading. When children have positive attitudes toward reading, they are intrinsically motivated to do it more often (with a more capable person reading to them until they can read on their own), and ultimately this will influence what children learn about literacy.

There has been a great deal of past research examining the reasons why family shared book reading is particularly facilitative for young children. In 1989, two researchers, Dorothy Strickland and Denny Taylor, came to the conclusion that there are several important conditions parents should create when reading with their children; they included an environment that is child-centered, giving children a greater choice over topics and more control over how the book reading proceeds, an atmosphere that fosters success, and a meaningful/interesting context.

Kathryn Edmunds and Kathryn Bauserman, two other researchers, were very interested in children's affect toward reading. The many negative comments about reading they heard from elementary school students prompted them to go to the source; in 2006, they conducted research in which they asked school-aged children what motivated them to read. Edmunds and Bauserman's findings were very similar to the conclusions of the other early childhood researchers about what motivates children to read: child-selected books, books that are personally interesting, various types of books, easy access, and the active involvement of others when they read.

This is consistent with the *interests-first perspective*—the belief that children are drawn into an activity because of personal interests. As they engage in these activities over and over again, they develop knowledge and skills; subsequently, they begin to feel good about what they are doing, become motivated to do so more often, and develop a higher self-efficacy toward this task. As stated in chapter 1, self-efficacy is the belief one has about his or her ability to learn and perform during any given task, and in this case, the ability to read. Children with low self-efficacy often will not attempt a literacy task because they believe they will not be successful (Walker 2003) and their failure will only cause further emotional anxiety (Pajares 2003).

So during book reading, parents should think about how they create environments that facilitate a pleasurable reading experience that is interesting to their children. Taking the time to select books your children will love and also asking your children to select the books they want read to them is critical. Creating a wonderfully warm and positive environment is also critical.

TWO SIMILAR SHARED STORYBOOK READING EVENTS— TWO DIFFERENT CHILD EXPERIENCES

In order to emphasize the importance of creating the *just right* learning environment when reading to your children, below is a description of two mother-child pairs during shared book reading (with their three-and-a-half-year-old children). The first mother appears to have captured many of the components researchers believe are important, while the second parent, although definitely well-intentioned, seems to have missed the boat regarding those qualities that are most important when creating an engaging learning environment so critical to children's emotional feelings toward reading.

Scenario #1

Rita, the mom, and Amy sat on an oversized couch in the living room during each of these readings. From the start, Amy was very enthusiastic that story time would be occurring with her mom, and it was clear that shared book reading was part of their daily routine. Before Rita read to Amy, she either asked Amy where she wanted to sit, or Amy sat on Rita's lap. Rita positioned the book so that Amy had a clear view of the illustrations and was close enough to reach the book to turn a page or point to a picture or word.

When selecting a book, Rita thumbed through the pile given her, selected a few, and then asked her daughter's opinion. Four books were selected: *If You Give a Mouse a Cookie* by Laura Joffe Numeroff was selected because it was a book Amy had asked to take out of the library; *Will I Have a Friend* by Miriam Cohen was selected because Rita was thinking of changing Amy's preschool; and *The Berenstain Bears and the Big Road Race* and *The Berenstain Bears and The Spooky Old Tree,* both by Stan and Jan Berenstain, were selected because Amy loved Berenstain Bear books. They also shared with me that recently Rita had taken Amy to see the play *The Spooky Old Tree.*

Throughout the reading, Rita also engaged in what can be described as *tender loving care* behaviors such as rubbing Amy's leg or arm, holding her, and smiling at her. Rita always spoke in a calm manner as she tried to settle Amy down. While Amy literally jumped on the couch with excitement and swung her legs in the air before each storybook reading, once Rita began reading, Amy listened intently (although sometimes standing), responding to both the words and the pictures in the story. If Amy started to turn the page, Rita encouraged her to continue by asking, "Do you want to turn the next page?" These book readings ended with Amy asking to read more. Amy also ran up to her room to retrieve one of her favorite books from her bedroom library to share.

Scenario #2

Joanne (the mom) and Michael's shared book reading sessions took place at the dining table. Michael was not eager to have his mother read to him during these visits. He wanted to play with his toys and his older brother and had to be coaxed by his mom into participating by getting a reward (e.g., "You will be able to go out and play" and "You will be able to use the computer").

Joanne selected the four storybooks based on the covers and titles of the books. She did not open the books. Joanne didn't ask Michael for assistance, and in fact, Michael was not in the room during her selection. She decided on *The Baby Blue Cat and the Whole Batch of Cookies* by Ainslie Pryor, *Where's My Teddy?* by Jez Alborough, *Will I Have a Friend?* by Miriam Cohen*,* and *The Cow That Went Oink* by Bernard Most.

Joanne positioned the storybooks so that the illustrations could be clearly viewed by Michael. She wrapped her arms around Michael and held the book in front of him like a harness to keep him from climbing off her lap. For each shared book reading, Joanne first read the title and author from the cover. For two of the shared book readings, Michael turned the pages, but he consistently turned the pages before Joanne was finished reading. Several times Joanne reprimanded him for not listening and directed Michael to turn the page at the appropriate time. Finally, she stopped him, and took over the task of turning the pages.

During the second visit, when Joanne read the third and fourth books, Michael was very disruptive, and clearly he had no interest in reading. Michael wanted to play with his brother Frank, so Joanne asked Frank to be a part of the shared book reading as a way of encouraging Michael and including Frank (which was a great idea, or so one would think). However, Frank quickly became bored and began fidgeting. Joanne ended up reprimanding Frank and sending him to his room to play.

Michael attempted to follow, but Joanne grabbed him by the arm, and sat Michael back on her lap, and said, "Oh no, you're not going anywhere." Michael squirmed on and off for the rest of the shared book reading and whined for several minutes. When Michael tried to get away, Joanne spoke in a harsh tone, making statements like, "I want you to do story time or you're not going to do the computer. The computer is going nowhere. You have to read these books first."

Frustrated, Joanne later shared that these are usual happenings during their shared book reading. She explained that either it is a fight to get Michael to sit and listen or Frank (Michael's brother) is looking for her attention, and so he disrupts them. Joanne seemed to view this time with Michael as an important task (or chore) that needed to be completed. At one point she stated, "Come on Michael, we have to read now. . . . Only two more books and we're done."

Reflecting on these two shared book reading experiences is critical: *Which scenario is a closer representation of your shared book reading time with your children? What type of atmosphere do you create when you are reading to/with your children?*

LET'S REVIEW

Remember shared book reading should illuminate your child's passionate, personal interests and topic-specific reading. Let's learn from these two scenarios and review by creating a "To Do" list when engaging in shared book reading with your children.

"To Dos" to Remember:

- Find a cozy and natural place to cuddle and read (e.g., a soft couch, a big reading chair, outdoors). The dining room table is not cozy and should be saved for Sunday dinner.
- Listen to your children throughout the day as they talk about their likes and dislikes. This will guide the type of books you select at bookstores and the library.
- Provide your children with several book choices, and praise them for the book they selected, even if you have read that same book a hundred times or you believe the book is a terrible choice!
- Demonstrate to your children that reading should be viewed as pleasurable by all. Don't demonstrate to your children that reading is work or a chore.
- Make each shared book reading a loving and warm part of your daily routine. Relax—this is a time to enjoy with no stress, and it is okay if your children don't sit perfectly still. They are young!
- Think about how you position the book. Have you placed the book in front of your children so they can see the left to right directionality of reading and turning of the pages from beginning to end?
- Select a more interesting book, IF your children begin showing little interest in a book you are reading to them; there is no reason why you MUST finish reading that book.
- Pick a time of day to read when your children won't be distracted by other activities in which they might be interested. Shared book reading should not be in competition with other pleasurable activities.
- Connect the topics of the books with your children's real-life experiences.
- Encourage your children to *sample the text* by flipping through and examining some of the illustrations to see if they are interested in this book.

- Section off a part of your children's room just for books, that is, create a bedroom library and make it a *special* place.
- Place books in other rooms in the house, such as a playroom and the living room. This will make it more likely that children will select a book to look through and pretend read.

These are general recommendations worthy of any shared book reading. These simple guidelines would have fostered more successful reading experiences with Joanne and Michael, and they will work for you and your children too!

In concluding this chapter, it is important to again reference one of the conditions of learning from Brian Cambourne (1988), located in chapter 1, and that is, in order for the learning process to take place, children need to be actively involved and engaged in the activity. Children must take ownership, be interested, and enjoy the reading experience. It is that simple. Think about it—all people are much more motivated when actively involved in doing any task, and they will repeat this task over and over, if they are in charge, if they are interested, and if it is enjoyable to them! Children are no different. So—*if your child does not like carrots, then perhaps it is time to try a different vegetable!*

Chapter Five

A Recipe for Shared Book Reading Ensures a Delicious Outcome

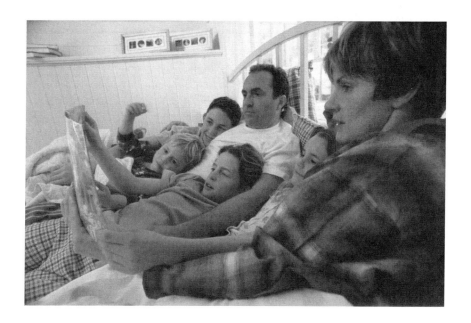

The importance of process should not be undervalued; a successful outcome is always based on the actions carried out leading up to the final product. Therefore, to improve a product, one must reflect on the manner in which it was completed. Case in point:

Sunday dinner is a tradition that lives on in this family, and Alexandra has proudly taken on much of the cooking each week. To keep meals interesting, she likes to try a variety of dinners, but she seems to follow very similar actions every Sunday morning, which involve three stages: **prepping** to make the meal**, engaging** in the actual cooking of the meal, and **concluding** with eating the meal. She has watched her favorite chefs, like Bobby Flay and Ina Garten, who also seem to follow these same generic cooking behaviors.

First is the **prep** to cook stage. Last week, for the first time, Alexandra cooked beef short ribs and polenta. Alexandra began by thinking about other meals she had made that were similar and previewing some old and new recipes. With a little help from Myrecipes.com, she quickly added to her knowledge. By previewing, Alexandra gathered additional ideas for the ingredients and cookware that would be needed. She also predicted that the meal would take approximately three hours and could be cooked similarly to how she previously cooked pork ribs. She often pulls together an adaptation of something she has tried before or seen another family member cook.

Second is to **engage** in the actual cooking. With making beef short ribs, Alexandra continued to connect her knowledge of making pork ribs to beef short ribs and seasoned and seared the meat, which worked out well, thus confirming her idea that beef short ribs and pork ribs can be cooked in a similar manner. Alexandra had never made polenta, but based on her new knowledge, she learned it would only take five minutes, and it seemed to be very much like rice. She, therefore, predicted that adding parmesan cheese and pancetta to her polenta would taste better. Within the recipe that was guiding her, Alexandra came to an unfamiliar word, *gremolata*. However, she then recalled that she had heard this word during a recent trip to Italy and realized it was probably pronounced "grem-OH-la-TA." There was also an illustration of the finished product, so Alexandra predicted gremolata was some type of Italian parsley topping and made her own version of it.

Alexandra also tasted her food over and over again, almost to the point where she was full by the time the family sat down to dinner! Monitoring one's cooking is the sign of any great chef. (Most also enjoy a glass of wine!) When making the beef short ribs, it was critical to monitor the ribs until the meat was so tender that it was falling off the bone with a fork. Sometimes, when she gave her food the taste test, Alexandra fixed it up, like by adding liquid, salt, or other seasonings to her dish.

Finally, Alexandra **concludes** the cooking process by bringing the family together to eat as she waits for reactions from them. Every Sunday, there is a discussion about what the family liked best, and sometimes they actually go back and compare the current meal to meals of the past. Alexandra has a recipe journal where she records what worked and how she could make the meal better next time. The product, the beef short ribs over polenta, was delicious!

IT'S A LITTLE LIKE ORCHESTRATING A SUNDAY DINNER

By now you must have realized that each personal story shared with you has some connection to reading, so why the Sunday dinner story? Like successful chefs, as parents who are their children's first literacy teachers, you also need to follow a *routine of actions* or an *instructional guide* during your shared book experience, which is very similar to effective cooking; it is crucial that you model and facilitate effective *prepping*, *engaging*, and *concluding* reading behaviors as you act as mediators during every shared book reading experience.

The chart below represents some of the most important reading behaviors that will be addressed in chapters 6, 7, and 8. These are musts when you read with your children, and once they are explained to you step by step, you will easily be able to find the similarities between a cooking routine of actions and a shared book reading routine of actions.

SHARED BOOK READING ROUTINE OF ACTIONS FOR SUCCESS!

PREP:

- **Preview** the Cover and/or the Book
- **Activate and Build** Background Knowledge
- **Predict** What Will Be Read
- **Set** a Purpose

ENGAGE:

- **Confirm** and Make New Predictions
- **Relate** New Ideas to Known
- **Connect** Letters/Sounds/Words to Context and Illustrations
- **Monitor** Understanding

CONCLUDE:

- **Discuss** your Child's Personal Reaction
- **Write** a Joint Reader Response
- **Identify** What Was Done Well
- **Enjoy** the Moment

As mentioned in chapter 3, there are two major tasks children must learn as they move from emergent to conventional reading: *decoding* and *comprehension*. Within this routine of actions, parents mediate reading behaviors that will focus on decoding as well as comprehension. In the coming chapters, decoding behaviors that are mediated by the parent will be referred to as *print-based instruction* and comprehension behaviors that are mediated by the parent will be referred to as *meaning-based instruction.*

An example of print-based instruction might be when a parent points to the beginning letter of a word and says, "Look, this word (or picture) begins with the same letter as your name Paul." A meaning-based behavior might be when a parent says, "Let's look at this illustration and see if we can find out what is going to happen next."

Remember the first goal you have as parents is to ensure that your children view reading as constructing meaning, not decoding text. Therefore, throughout these chapters, you will see a strong emphasis on this very important aspect. All too often educators have worked with struggling readers who sound fluent, meaning they can decode beautifully, but they have no clue what they are reading; there is little comprehension. (For Your Information: Children with this characteristic are frequently referred to as *word callers*.)

When these children are asked "What is reading?" and "Who is the best reader in your class?" they often respond, "Reading is sounding good," and "Jaime is a good reader because she can read all these hard words." This limited view of reading is sometimes the result of children's instructional history, that is, too much of a focus on the letter-sound relationship, without *connecting* it to the construction of meaning.

This is not done only in the home; many preschool programs are based on learning letters and sounds, but miss this very important and crucial piece: connecting it to understanding what is being read! If you are in disagreement with this belief, think back to how children learn oral language. Parents do *not* instruct their youngsters on every sound within every word in isolation; this would be ridiculous. They *do* learn to understand and speak because they hear and practice language in the context of authentic, *meaningful* oral text. To be clear, the decoding component should not be neglected; however, learning how to decode must be connected to the construction of meaning. This *is* effective instruction.

LET'S REVIEW

The ultimate goal of cooking is the finished product, a delicious meal. In accordance with this, the ultimate goal of reading is the finished product, comprehension. In both cases, we will not complete our goal successfully if we do not engage in effective behaviors or actions during the process of cooking or the process of reading. If our end product is not successful, we must go back and review the actions in which we engaged.

As parents nourish their children's reading development, they must act as mediators, that is, focus their children on a series of reading actions, which have been grouped into three stages: **PREP** *(before reading)*, **ENGAGE** *(during reading)*, and **CONCLUDE** *(after reading)*. Eventually, young children are able to do this on their own. While there are many reading behaviors, this parent workshop has been limited to twelve that are critical for youngsters to possess in order to be proficient readers.

Children will begin to define reading based on the experiences parents practice with them in the home. Rather than providing an explanation of reading skills, parents should facilitate the acquisition of reading through exposure, modeling, and the process of practicing through trial and error in natural settings. Children's perceptions and how they approach reading and view themselves as readers are acquired through the reading practices that are emphasized during shared book reading; this includes both meaning-based and print-based behaviors. Your children will internalize those strategies you spend a lot of time on during your interactive reading, and these behaviors will become part of your children's repertoire as they move toward conventional reading. Your ultimate goal is for your children to become strategic readers so let us get started with ***prepping*** *to read*!

Chapter Six

PREP Is the First Step!

So often we want to jump in and engage in the actual task rather than take the time to prepare first. Then we wonder why we were not successful. For example, you have all probably heard someone profess, "I am not good at putting things together," but is this really accurate? Or is it a lack of **prepping**? Case in point:

When Alexandra turned one, her dad and mom decided to throw a big birthday party in the backyard with family and friends. It would be simple—hamburgers, hotdogs, and roasted corn on the cob. The problem was they had no barbecue.

So, her dad rushed out the day before and bought a huge gas grill; however, there was no time for Home Depot to assemble it. Dad thought, "How difficult could this be?" Well, if you didn't already know this, gas grills have many, many parts, along with a rather large manual, and there was little time to read through pages of directions. Dad was not a "handyman" as his mother would say, but he believed he was up for the challenge.

Dad believed skimming the manual would suffice, but after flipping through a few pages, he became impatient, and it was getting late, so he began pulling the parts out of the box and using some of the diagrams instead of first reading the instructions. Can you picture what the patio looked like hours later? Screws, tools, and parts were all over the place, and at midnight, Dad gave up.

Rather than hamburgers and hotdogs, six-foot heroes and salads were served at the birthday party, and "mom and dad" ended up paying someone the following week to bring some new parts and build the grill. Although most of us are eager to actually get started doing whatever we want to do, preparation is a critical step; it is the foundation for the task itself. It sets us up for success . . . or failure.

Prepping is equally important for readers. Hence, parents must get their children ready to read before any shared book reading; this will set them up for success! Books that interest and are suitable for your child, as stated in chapter 4, must be considered first. Then, as mediators of your children's reading, four **PREP** actions that were outlined for you to follow in chapter 5 should be followed. These four actions are connected to one another in a continuous cycle where each depends on the other.

PREVIEW THE COVER AND/OR THE BOOK

How do parents teach their children to do this? One of the best ways to guide your children to actively participate in reading is to *Preview the Cover and/or*

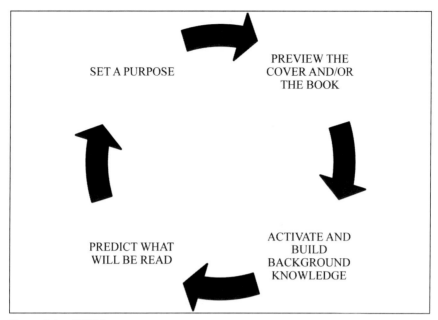

Figure 6.1.   PREP Stage

the Book, component 1 in the **PREP** stage. This can easily be done by reading the title of the book, looking at the illustrations on the cover, and then if your child is developmentally ready and interested, taking a *picture walk* (Goldenberg 1991) through the book. A picture walk is quite simple; it is basically a visual walk through the book, similar to looking at your surroundings when you walk through a park and talk about what you are seeing with your children. All you need to do is flip through the pages, focusing on some of the illustrations and graphics and talking about these key or *tricky* ideas that your children will encounter in the text.

How will you know when you should engage in only previewing the cover illustrations and title of the book, and when you should actually engage in a more advanced picture walk preview? As previously mentioned throughout this book, get to *know* your child's ability level and interests. Some children by the age of three enjoy not only previewing the cover, but also flipping through the pages to see what the book is about. For other children, this can be counterproductive; it is too much for them.

So Parents. *know* your children and the books. If the book is too lengthy or taking a picture walk will reveal a surprise ending, just looking at the cover (and maybe the first few pages) is more appropriate. The age of your child will also guide you; it makes sense that for younger children, a preview of the entire book will be ineffective. Parents, any time your child is resisting an activity, stop and move on. All reading activities should be enjoyable!

Previewing will be useful for two reasons. First, it *activates* your children's *background knowledge* about specific topics so they can now *relate to the text*. For example, if the book is titled *All about Preschool*, by your focusing on the illustrations and talking about your children's own experiences in preschool, it sets up their brains to relate the information you will read to them with what they already know. In addition, this will also *build* on your children's background knowledge if they do not know a great deal about a topic, or there are some *tricky* or confusing concepts.

Also, assess your children while *Previewing*. If you recall, in chapter 1 the ideas of two educational/cognitive psychologists, Lev Vygotsky (1978) and Jerome Bruner (1977) were introduced. One very important principle of Vygotsky's thinking in regard to learning was that learning cannot take place unless there is a situation where, one, the child is engaged in an activity that is too difficult to complete on his or her own, and two, the child's behaviors are supported by another capable individual where he or she will meet with success (Dixon-Krauss 1996). (For Your Information: This is termed *operating within a child's zone of proximal development.*)

This means through social interaction, parents engage in ongoing assessment of their children's abilities, and as Bruner suggested, it is critical that parents act as supports, scaffolding children's abilities and raising expectations as their children develop. *Previewing* the book is the perfect time to begin evaluating your children's abilities, as you begin to establish this *zone* (that is, children meeting with success with the help of a more capable individual) in order to guide the upcoming shared book reading.

ACTIVATE AND BUILD BACKGROUND KNOWLEDGE

The action to *Activate and Build Background Knowledge*, the second component of the **PREP** stage, is critical because all learning, that is, all construction of meaning, is based on relating new ideas to known. This is important because the known information that is already a part of your child's thinking anchors the new ideas that will be found in the text. You are also facilitating your child's ability to differentiate more relevant from less relevant information in relation to what will be read.

Let us clarify this *before reading* behavior and how it relates to actual reading with an example. When reading the book *All about Preschool,* assume there is an illustration showing children painting pictures with blue, red, and yellow paint. It would be beneficial for a parent to discuss these paints during a picture walk with a brief discussion because they are relevant to the story. Now, fast forward to the **ENGAGE** stage (*during reading*). As the parent actually reads the text "The children gathered around the table with blue, red, and yellow paint," the parent might point to these color words, *blue, red*, and *yellow,* recalling the picture walk. This fosters a connection between the child's background knowledge about painting as well as his or her oral language of these color words and the printed text. So you can see how behaviors during the **PREP** stage will be supportive of children's reading during the **ENGAGE** stage.

Recall from chapter 3 that the more background knowledge children bring to the text, the greater chance they will *predict* what the next sentence, next word, or next page will be. So when children are conventionally reading, they won't spend too much time decoding (and overloading their brains or cognitive capacity) and will be able to attend to meaning. So before children begin reading, helping them bring their background knowledge about the topic front and center is critical to the du*ring reading* success. Additionally, as previously mentioned, by previewing and activating prior knowledge, parents can informally assess if there are gaps in their children's schema, and build on it when necessary.

PREDICT WHAT WILL BE READ

By *previewing* and *activating/building background knowledge*, your children's brains now have a framework for the reading, and they can easily engage in the third **PREP** action, *Predict What Will Be Read*. A reader's ability to *predict* is the basis of all comprehension.

To review, proficient readers make predictions based on their background knowledge, so by previewing the cover and/or the book, you have activated and built your children's background knowledge in order for them to make logical guesses. They will learn to make predictions almost immediately after they begin previewing the book because you have naturally modeled making predictions when you read to them and when you invited them to also make predictions.

Using the *All about Preschool* book example, a dad might ask his son, "What do you think this book is going to be about? Or "What do you think the children will be doing at this preschool?" Clearly, the child will utilize knowledge about preschools that was activated during the picture walk and his own personal experiences to answer these questions. The parent has begun the predicting-confirming cycle that is a part of the reading process and will be continued when the actual reading occurs during the **ENGAGE** stage.

Moreover, this parent has naturally directed his child to the fourth component in the **PREP** cycle because these prediction questions will *set a purpose* for the reading. The goal or purpose will be to see if these predictions are true or not once the reading takes place. Once again, you see the strong connection between the **PREP** and **ENGAGE** stages.

SET A PURPOSE

Why is it important to guide your children to *set a purpose* when reading? There are several objectives. Setting a purpose is critical to strategic reading because it sets goals for the task in which your children are about to engage. By setting a goal(s), it motivates your children to find out about something, and it directs your children's thinking to focus on specific, relevant information once they do begin reading, or in this instance, when you read with them. Not all information is created equally, so proficient readers *set a purpose* for reading to guide their brains to focus on only the information that is important for understanding.

Think about setting a purpose as a way to set up *learning intentions* for your children. With anything we do, we must be selective in what we decide to attend to and what we leave behind. If not, we will overload our memory, with little construction of meaning and recall. An analogy might be when a college student is trying to study for a test, but instead of thinking, "What is the most important information to study?" he or she tries to cram in every single idea the professor has presented over several weeks and ultimately learns very little.

Setting purposes for reading predisposes your children to think about the most important ideas in the text. Because these ideas will receive more attention, there is a greater chance that this information will be understood and remembered better. It is therefore important to note that the attention a reader gives to any text, or in this case how you as the mediator guide your child to attend to a specific purpose, has to do with perspective.

One rather well-known study that demonstrates this was conducted by Goetz, Schallert, Reynolds, and Radin in 1983. During their investigation, they asked different groups of people to read a story about two boys playing hooky from school and engaging in antics throughout the day. Before reading, they asked policemen to take the perspective of a burglar and the real estate agents to take the perspective of a prospective homeowner. They didn't give any perspective to the group of college students.

As you might have predicted, the policemen playing the role of burglar recalled information related to where money was kept and that there was a large television, whereas the real estate agents recalled the leaky roof and a spacious estate. Clearly, this shows that your child's background knowledge and your ability to explicitly guide your child to set purposes for the shared book reading is actually providing him or her with a particular perspective and will influence what your child understands and recalls in the text.

Thus, all four **PREP** actions are orchestrated together; rather than as isolated actions, they are interrelated reading behaviors. As you will see when these behaviors are modeled for you in detail on the next few pages, these four steps aren't done sequentially, but rather it is a back and forth of behaviors depending on the unique context of the shared reading event and your children's responses. It becomes part of your natural conversation as you share reading with your children.

ACTION!

It is time to model the four **PREP** behaviors, *Preview the Book, Activate/ Build Background Knowledge, Predict What Will Be Read, and Set a Purpose* in order to provide a better understanding of the previous section of this chapter. The children's book, *A Wondrous World in My Head* (Voorhees 2013) will be used to demonstrate these four simple **PREP** behaviors. You can download this book in color by going to Amazon.com/Kindle; however, if you would rather not take the time right now, you can also view these pages in Appendix A. In addition to the extensive dialogue of the shared book reading experience, the specific **PREP** behaviors have been identified in brackets.

Let us set the stage. The shared book reading experience is with a four-year-old boy named Harrison. He is the nephew of the reader, so there is a high comfort level between the reader and the child, similar to how you would be with your children. Although it is a good practice to give Harrison a choice as to what book he wanted to read (sometimes giving him a "selected choice" by providing three or four books), for the purpose of this demonstration, he was asked if he would like to read a new book previously selected. He already possesses what would be considered a good *affect* or attitude toward reading because Harrison has had many positive experiences with books since he was born.

Next, establishing a *relaxing* place to sit is important; it was decided that the couch on the porch was *comfy* and there would be few distractions. The time of day that was selected for the shared book reading was when Harrison was not tired (or cranky), soon after he ate lunch. Harrison was handed the book as he settled in on the couch. Harrison quickly handed the book back and so together they snuggled close so the cover of the book could easily be viewed. At this point, the *picture walk* was facilitated.

Remember a picture walk is a way of *previewing* the book by flipping through and discussing each page before actually reading; it will set up a framework for your children by identifying relevant ideas/key concepts *and activating and building appropriate background knowledge*. You will also see how *predicting* and *setting a purpose* becomes a natural part of the process. Below is an edited transcript of the picture walk:

Kathy: (Pointing to the title on the cover) "Harrison, the name of this book is called *A Wondrous World in My Head.* Can you say this title?"

Harrison: (Saying it very slowly, with a little difficulty when pronouncing "Wondrous") "A Won-der-is World in My Head."

Kathy: "Yes, **Wondrous** (with emphasis) means to wonder or think about something. (Pointing to the illustration of the little boy's head on the cover) I bet this little boy has a lot of things he thinks about, just like you. Let's think about what he might be wondering . . . looks like different animals above his head! I think he is wondering about an elephant." [Previewing the cover; modeling as well as activating and building background knowledge about the word *wondrous* and book topic.]

Harrison: "And a lion (Smiling and pointing to the lion)."

Kathy: "Yes, that's great, Harrison. I am always thinking about what it would be like to be different things. Sometimes I wonder what it would be like to be a wiggly worm. Do you ever wonder what it would be like to be a wiggly worm (Kathy wiggles her body)?"

(Harrison and Kathy laugh) [Activate/building background knowledge about the book.]

Harrison: "Nooooo (smiling)."

Kathy: (Directing Harrison back to the cover) "And a kangaroo (pointing to the kangaroo). Let's look at the pictures in the book and see if we can figure out some of the other things this little boy is wondering about." [Activating/building background knowledge; setting the stage for predicting.]

Kathy: (Turning to the first page and pointing to the illustration) "Well, here is the little boy's head again. Let's see what might be going on in his head. (Turning the next page and pointing to the illustration) Look, what is that?" [Activating/building background knowledge]

Harrison: "That's a bug!"

Kathy: "That's right. It looks like an ant. (Pointing to the illustration) And what is that?"

Harrison: "That's a foot."

Kathy: "Yes, that's right, with a very big toe that the ant is crawling on." [Activating/building background knowledge]

Kathy: (Previewing the next two pages and pointing to the illustrations) "And what is this animal?"

Harrison: "That's a dog."

Kathy: "Did you ever wonder what it would be like to be your dog Bella?" [Encouraging Harrison to activate his own background knowledge and make connections]

Harrison: (Laughing) "Nooooo."

Kathy: "Bella is little, and I can imagine it must be fun to lie on everyone's lap and jump on the couch." [Modeling activating background knowledge and relating it to new information he will encounter in the book]

Kathy: (Previewing the next two pages and pointing to the illustrations) "And what is this a picture of?"

Harrison: (shrugs his shoulders)

Kathy: "That's a **kangaroo**! (With emphasis) Remember I mentioned this animal from the cover. [Building background knowledge] (Pointing to the illustration of the kangaroo jumping) Kangaroos can jump really high. How high can you jump?" [Encouraging activating his background knowledge about jumping and relating it to a kangaroo]

(Harrison jumps off the couch and starts hopping around the room) [Relating the background knowledge provided about kangaroos to his existing background knowledge about jumping]

Kathy: (Turning the next page but covering the illustration except for the lion's tail) "Before I show you the next page, what do you think this little boy is going to wonder about next?" [Encouraging predicting]

Harrison: "A cat."

Kathy: "Let's find out. (Previewing the next two pages) Well that was really close. It is a kind of cat . . . it is a lion. ROAR!" [Disconfirming his prediction and activating and building his background knowledge]

Harrison: (Loudly) "***ROAR!***"

Kathy: (Before turning the page) "What do you think we are going to see on the next page? [Encouraging predicting]

(Showing part of the illustration) This animal is VERY TALL!" [Encouraging predicting]

Harrison: "A giraffe!"

Kathy: "That's right!" [Confirming his prediction]

Kathy: (Previewing the next two pages and pointing to the illustrations) "I'm not sure you ever saw one of these?"

Harrison: (Shakes his head "no")

Kathy: "They have these sharp needles called quills on their backs. This animal is a porcupine . . . just like pine tree needles that we have in the backyard." [Building/activating background knowledge by connecting it to this new information] (Pointing out the window to the pine tree)

Kathy: "What will we see on the next page?" [Encouraging predicting]

Harrison: "I don't know . . . maybe a horse."

Kathy: (Previewing the next two pages)

Harrison: "An elephant!" [Harrison disconfirms his prediction.]

Kathy: "Yes!"

Harrison: "That is a big elephant! They are big and have trunks!" [Activating his background knowledge without a prompt]

Kathy: (Pointing to the illustration of the elephant on the barge) "Yes, and this boat over here is called a **barge** (with emphasis)! It carries all sorts of big things, like crates of food, tools, cars. Things they call **freight** (with emphasis). This boat is like the freight trains you play with at your house." [Activating/building background knowledge by relating it to something in Harrison's life—Harrison has several trains and train tracks at home]

Kathy: (Turning to the next two pages) "And here is a **sly** (with emphasis and hesitation) . . . fox. [Hesitating in order to see if Harrison can predict the next animal based on the illustration) They are very smart." [Activating/building background knowledge]

(Turning to the next two pages and pointing to the illustrations)

Harrison: "I know what they are . . . that's a lightning bug. I caught one of them and put it in a jar." [Harrison has caught on to these reading behaviors being modeled and is actively engaging in the illustrations; he is activating and connecting the illustrations to his background knowledge]

Kathy: "I **wonder** (with emphasis) what it would be like to be able to light up like a light bulb!" (Modeling relating background knowledge to the text/ illustrations)

Harrison: "That would be fun."

Kathy: "That would be fun. (Turning to the last two pages and pointing to the final illustration) Looks like this boy is very happy. He has a big smile on his face. Why do you think he is so happy?" [Encouraging predicting and setting a purpose]

Harrison: (Shrugging his shoulders)

Kathy: "Maybe he is happy because he has a good imagination." [Modeling predicting]

Harrison: "Yeah."

Kathy: "Do you think he might be happy because he can imagine being all these things?" [Modeling predicting and setting a purpose for reading the book]

Harrison: (Shakes his head yes)

Kathy: "I think we are going to have to read the book and find out why he is so happy at the end of the book. [Modeling setting a purpose for reading the book] Do you want to read the book?"

Harrison: "Yeah." (Smiles)

Kathy: "Okay, so can you turn to the first page [*For Your Information: By asking Harrison to do this, book handling behaviors are being encouraged*], and let's see what we find out about why this boy is so happy." [Restating setting a purpose for the reading]

(Harrison turns to the beginning of the book)

This concludes the **PREP** actions for Harrison. As you review the above transcript, what aspects of these actions are you focused on? What questions come to mind in regard to this *before reading* stage?

LET'S REVIEW

Although the above dialogue may appear lengthy as you read through it; it actually took about five minutes or less to complete. Also, many examples of parent reading behaviors are included in order to foster a greater understanding of **PREP** behaviors. (Remember, the age, developmental level, and interest of your child will guide you to engage in either previewing the cover or conducting a partial or complete picture walk.) As with any task, the **PREP** stage includes probably the most important actions we can take to ensure a successful outcome.

A picture walk should be a quick activity, and as you can see, it is a way to model and engage your children in the four interrelated **PREP** steps: *Preview the Book* in order to *Build and Activate Background Knowledge*, which in turn allows readers to *Predict What Will Be Read*, and this *Sets a Purpose* for the reading so your children pay attention to specific aspects of the book. These actions foster those reading behaviors mentioned in chapter 3 when the reading process was explained.

You, as the mediator of your children's learning, will need to model these **PREP** actions over and over again before your children will begin taking over these behaviors. If you make this part of your shared book reading routine, your children will soon begin to do this before you have a chance to prompt them! Eventually, it will become part of their pretend reading behaviors, and finally, it will transfer over to conventional reading, which is EXACTLY what you want to happen! Please try **prep**ping your children today when you read to them through a picture walk, or by previewing the cover, with whatever book your children have selected. Do not worry about being perfect mediators; you will naturally get better as you develop your own interactive behaviors, so just enjoy it. Now, it is time to move on to the next stage, which is to **ENGAGE** in the actual reading event.

Chapter Seven

ENGAGE: Be a Lore, Not a Bore!

Engagement is critical to all learning, at any level, as stated in chapter 1 of this book. One must be a part of the learning process of any task in order for a positive outcome to occur. And this positive outcome motivates humans to want to do it again and again. Case in point:

Thinking back to your schooling, you can probably come up with the one teacher who could make the most interesting topic put you to sleep. Mr. Bodem, a sixth-grade science teacher, comes to my mind—monotone, disconnected from his students, uninteresting. He rarely allowed his students to have any interaction and certainly the subject matter should have included many hands-on experiments, which the class did not do. Even the most academic students didn't achieve an *A* and hated attending class. Mr. Bodem's classes were passive recipients of any information he imparted and, for sure, most students never picked up their textbook at home. Many classmates vowed to never continue their studies in this area.

But Mr. Pulcino, the math teacher in the same school, was beloved by all students! One would think that math class would be a bore, but he captured everyone's attention each day—animated, standing on desks as he demonstrated abstract ideas, connecting stories and mottos to the subject matter, and ensuring that his students understood one concept before moving on to the next. eH neve etorw sdrow sdrawkcab ot barg ruo noitnetta. This certainly forced our brains to be active if we started to lose concentration! (FYI: The sentence says, "He even wrote words backwards to grab our attention.") Did it just work with you? (Mr. Pulcino actually had such an influence on me that I earned a minor in mathematics in college.)

So what is the point? As mediators of your children's reading, during the actual *reading stage*, your goal is to demonstrate **ENGAGE** actions that will foster excitement and active learning for your children.

Before presenting specific **ENGAGE** reading actions in detail, it is important to review the importance of parents' *affective behaviors,* that is, the emotions and desires parents demonstrate during the shared book reading, which influence children's actions. First, be sure your child shares in the responsibilities and is an equal partner. This could be as simple as allowing your child to share in holding the book or perhaps asking your child to turn the pages. Most importantly, be sure the book is in front of both of you.

Now, get your reading voice ready! Children's picture books are written by the most gifted writers and illustrated by the most talented artists; however, they are not there to ensure their work is presented at its best. So parents, your job is to bring these books to life. Be **animated**, act out parts, **change the**

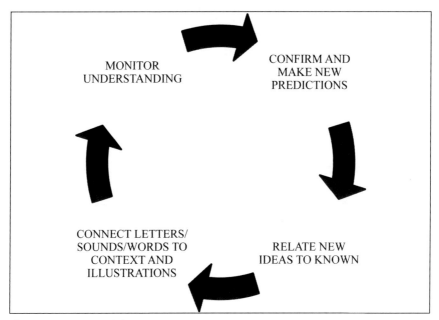

Figure 7.1. ENGAGE Stage

tone of your voice, s-l-o-w your voice down, speed it up, whisper, **RAISE YOUR VOICE LEVEL . . .** all at appropriate times, of course. Sometimes you will be tired, especially after a long day, but your enthusiasm and ability to create an interesting shared book reading will make the difference!

The four **ENGAGE** actions presented in chapter 5 will also facilitate an active and positive shared book reading experience. As with the **PREP** actions, these four **ENGAGE** actions are connected to one another and should be viewed in a continuous cycle where each depends on the other in a back-and-forth motion, rather than viewed sequentially.

CONFIRM AND MAKE NEW PREDICTIONS

Think of reading as a mental and language guessing game! In the previous chapter, the idea to predict what the book will be about was presented as part of the *before reading* actions. Now that the reading has begun, it is equally important to *confirm* or disconfirm the original predictions and *make new predictions*. Back to the *All about Preschool* book example: Before reading (**PREP** stage) a mother might ask her son, "What do you think these children will be doing at this preschool?" and the little boy might respond, "coloring, singing, playing, and having circle time."

Now during reading, when the mother reads text related to this, like "All the children gathered around the piano and sang their favorite songs. Laura sang the loudest," the mother, as a mediator, must be sure to explicitly remind her son of this prediction. For instance, she might say "Remember when you said that the children will be coloring, singing, playing, and having circle time? You were right about singing, because here they are around the piano." By doing this, parents are encouraging their children to not only make predictions but *actively confirm* these predictions.

Here is a reminder from chapter 3: To be a proficient reader, one must make predictions by utilizing prior knowledge that one has about a topic and then see if these predictions make sense, that is, occur, by actually reading the text. Or you must disconfirm, if this is not what the author presents in the text. Parents can help children do this at an *idea level* (as with the example of children singing around the piano), but also at a word level.

For example, as a dad is reading *All about Preschool* to his daughter, he might read, "All the children were so excited and ran to the window to watch the rain turn into. . . . " but instead of reading the word "snow," he pauses and perhaps starts pronouncing "ssss . . . sssnnn" sounds, pointing to the word "snow" and pointing to the illustration of the snow coming down outside the window. By engaging in this prediction reading action, he is encouraging his child to make a prediction based on the context of the story, specifically the sentence and illustration, as well as fostering his daughter to actively use her knowledge of oral language and sounds and connecting it to the printed word, "snow."

If parents make these pauses at appropriate times (that is, when the contexts and illustrations support the predictions), they will see their children begin to jump in often to predict that next word. The parent confirms the prediction by just reading the word and acknowledging that it is accurate.

Sometimes children will predict an incorrect word or idea, and this is fine. It is not about always being right, it is about encouraging the *prediction-confirming/disconfirming* cycle. In order for the brain to stay active, readers need to activate their prior knowledge, make predictions, and seek out information from the text to see if these predictions were what the author intended or not. It forces the brain to focus on specific aspects of the text, as readers give their brains a direction so they do not get lost in a sea of words, but rather construct meaning.

Parents, therefore, at appropriate points in the story, model and also encourage children to make predictions and then confirm or disconfirm them as they learn more information. Questions like "What do you think will happen next?" or leaving out the last word of a sentence so your child can guess that word, are simple ways to encourage this cycle to continue at appropriate points during your shared book reading.

RELATE NEW IDEAS TO KNOWN

While explaining the prediction-confirming/disconfirming cycle, the second **ENGAGE** component, *Relate New Ideas to Known* was also indicated to you. Quite clearly, in order to make predictions, the reader needs to have some prior knowledge available to him or her. The examples of the preschool readings above exemplify this; children cannot predict what might occur in a preschool if they had never heard about, seen, or experienced a preschool. Also, as a reminder from the previous chapter, if your child does not have prior knowledge about a topic, you would begin building prior knowledge during the **PREP** stage.

Activating prior knowledge, however, is not enough. Readers must also relate their prior knowledge to the new information they are encountering in the text. This is how we learn anything, that is, we *relate new to known*. It makes sense that analogies work so well when one is learning a complex idea for the first time. While the action itself of relating new to known is the same for everyone, the specific information that is related will be unique for every reader based on his or her experiences. You know your children best, so you can facilitate making these new ideas to known connections!

In the *Confirm and Make New Predictions* section, it was explained how a parent could confirm the prediction a child made about singing at a preschool. Additionally, parents can now add to this proficient reading behavior of confirming by facilitating *relating new to known* actions. In this instance, the parent can first confirm the prediction, "Look, you were correct. Before you began reading you said that these children would be singing at their preschool, and here they are gathered around the piano singing."

However, then the parent can further the child's thinking by adding a question, like "Do you remember when you sat on the rug next to the piano and sang with the other children in Ms. Hemingway's class? Who was the loudest in your group . . . was it you?" By making this very simple comment, parents are actually connecting the new ideas in the text to the child's already existing schema (adding to a mental framework of a concept in the child's brain and thus solidifying what is happening in the story).

Here are a few prompts you can say *during reading* to guide you when facilitating new-to-known connections:

- This reminds me of when . . .
- This is similar to . . .
- This is very different from . . .
- Do you know anyone like this?
- Did you ever have an experience like this?
- Did you know anything about this (whatever subject/topic you might be reading about)?

These are just a few prompts, but in short, relate new information that you are reading about, whether it is fictional or factual information, to your children's and your experiences any way you can. There is no right or wrong manner to do this!

CONNECT LETTERS/SOUNDS/WORDS
TO CONTEXT AND ILLUSTRATIONS

The third **ENGAGE** component, *Connect Letters/Sounds/Words to Context and Illustrations*, cannot occur when separated from *predicting-confirming/disconfirming* behaviors and the *relating new to known* behaviors. Past observations of parents and young children seem to indicate that the richest shared book reading events were when parents (or teachers) emphasized the meaning of what was being read, but also connected meaning to language. Reading is understanding, but this cannot take place if children do not learn how to decode, so it is also important for parents to mediate print-based behaviors along with meaning-based behaviors.

This was also noted in the *Confirm and Make New Predictions* section with the example of a parent fostering the child's ability to predict the word "snow" by providing the child with the beginning sounds and connecting these beginning sounds to the text and illustration. Print-based behaviors are often a combination of nonverbal and verbal actions. These actions include, but are not limited to, the following:

- pointing to the words in a flowing motion under each sentence while reading to the child;
- pointing at specific words as they are being read, like RED paint, for emphasis;
- connecting the child's oral vocabulary with the print;
- comparing two or more words being read in terms of beginning or ending sounds;
- identifying rhyming words; and
- identifying a repeated line.

Some young reader picture books are more conducive to this type of print-based mediating behavior than others. These books are often called predictable books because they are written with some type of pattern. It might be a repeated line, as in Bill Martin Jr.'s book, *Polar Bear, Polar Bear What Do You Hear?*; a rhyming pattern, as in Mem Fox's book, *Time for Bed*; or a predictable plot, as in Laura Numeroff's book, *If You Give a Mouse a Cookie.*

These types of books help young children to quickly connect to the text because hearing these texts over and over again allows children to quickly memorize the text. Once the text is memorized, with the guidance of parents pointing to the words (in a slow sweeping motion), children make a voice to print match which is the transition to conventional reading.

It is up to parents to decide when it is the best time to intermittently provide these print-based behaviors. But this will not be arbitrary. The way the author has written the book will guide you. Besides the patterns previously mentioned, the author provides other clues for you, especially through the illustrations and font. Picture books include illustrations that closely match the text on that specific page and convey the most salient ideas.

Additionally, authors change the size and color of the font, as well as the position of words, for emphasis. One only has to look at *The Spooky Old Tree* and *The Big Road Race* by Stan and Jan Berenstain to see these words POP OUT at the reader. I think parents should think of themselves as being in partnerships with authors and illustrators. They have supplied you with their talents and now it is your responsibility to take it the rest of the way!

MONITOR UNDERSTANDING

One final and very important *during reading* mediating action also connects these other actions; this is *to monitor understanding* during reading. In psychological terms, this could be explained as developing your child's *internal locus of control*. Basically, it means that children should sense or believe that they control the outcome of the reading event—the outcome being comprehension. Once again, it is important to remember that some children may be ready to do this by the age of three while others may not be ready until they are four of even five years old. From the earliest age possible, however, parents need to facilitate *active* emergent readers.

"What the heck did I just read for the past few minutes?" is a feeling all readers have experienced while reading. You might be reading a newspaper article or book, or whatever, but instead of attending to the contents of the book, your mind takes a trip someplace else, or you just completely *zone out*. While you are zoning out, you are actually passively reading, and once you bring yourself back, you are engaging in active reading once again, that is, you are aware that you are not comprehending the text. (Has *zoning out* occurred while reading this book?)

Ongoing self-assessment of one's reading is key to proficient reading. Therefore, children's *state* of comprehension is vital. When parents ask, "Does this make sense?" and clarify any material that does not make sense, they are nurturing their child to be an active thinker. Children will learn to monitor their understanding (or be aware when they do not understand) and use fix-up strategies when they "don't get it!" This is a comment often stated by less proficient readers who read with little understanding, but then these type of readers just give up, rather than actively problem solve until they comprehend. It is critical to proficient reading for the reader to believe that he or she is in control of the outcome.

Returning one more time to the *All about Preschool* reading will demonstrate these self-monitoring behaviors more visibly. First, here is an example at a word level: The text said, "All the children gathered around the piano and sang their favorite songs. Laura sang the loudest!" But, instead of "loudest," the parent makes an error or what we call a *miscue,* and decodes the last word as "largest." This is a perfect opportunity for the parent to demonstrate self-monitoring behaviors by simply stating, "Wait, *largest,* doesn't make sense to me. Let me go back and look at that word again and reread this sentence." The parent then returns to the beginning of the sentence, rereads the sentence, correcting the miscue, and states that the corrected word makes more sense—an excellent self-monitoring behavior.

Sometimes it isn't a word that is read incorrectly. Perhaps self-monitoring is required after several pages about the overall content. During this type of situation, a parent might stop reading, and simply state the following: "For some reason I can't remember what happened on the last two pages, and they are important, so let's go back and reread those pages." Again, by using a simple *look-back,* parents are modeling fix-up strategies based on their monitoring of comprehension.

Or perhaps something that wasn't predicted by you or your child actually happens in the story. In these cases, the following prompts are appropriate:

- This isn't what I expected, I thought _____ would happen, but _____ happened instead.
- I do not understand this, let's go back and reread this part.
- I do not understand this, let's read ahead and see if we can figure this out.
- Let's stop and think about this for a minute . . . do you think the author meant _____?

When demonstrating these *think-aloud* self-monitoring behaviors, it is important to invite your child to join in by adding to your thoughts. A simple, "What do YOU think?" goes a long way. It is okay to *purposely* make a miscue (text error) or act confused about understanding in order to demonstrate these self-correcting behaviors. Shhhh, it will be our secret.

As you can see, self-monitoring/self-correcting cannot be separated from the first three actions. These are all *thinking* behaviors. We monitor our understanding of what we read when we

- test out or confirm-disconfirm our predictions;
- identify new information in the text and relate it to our prior knowledge; and
- connect our knowledge of sound/symbol relationships and our oral language with the context in order to decode words correctly or self-correct miscues (errors).

One behavior cannot exist without the other, and once again there is an orchestration of these behaviors that come together!

ACTION!

Let's join Harrison once again as the shared book reading of *A Wondrous World in My Head* continues. Recall, the *picture walk* had just been completed, and so it is now time to do the actual reading. If you remember, the picture walk ended with a prediction about why this boy was so happy at the end of the book; a prediction was modeled for Harrison: "Maybe he is happy because he has a good imagination."

Within this transcript, the four *during reading* actions will be pointed out in brackets as they occur. Recall, they include *Confirm and Make New Predictions, Relate New Ideas to Known, Connect Letters/Sounds/Words to Context and Illustrations, and Monitor Understanding.* These actions may not happen sequentially, but rather in a natural way based on the unique reading event that is occurring. Text in all capitals is used to identify the actual text of the book; words in **bold** are read with emphasis. Starting with the first page:

Kathy: "MY HEAD IS A WORLD OF WONDER. IT SETS ME FREE. THERE ARE SO MANY LIVING THINGS I WOULD LIKE TO BE. Harrison, let's look again at the animals above the boy's head. What do you see?" (Pointing to the illustrations of animals above the boy's head) [Activating prior knowledge in order to relate new to known]

Harrison: "I see an elephant, lion, and. . . . I forget that one (pointing to the kangaroo)."

Kathy: "That's a kangaroo!"

Kathy: (Turning page) "I WONDER WHAT IT WOULD BE LIKE TO BE AN **ANT**." (Pointing to the illustration of the ant)

(Next page) "CRAWLING SO **LOW**, I COULD RIDE YOUR BIG **TOE!** (Pointing to the illustration of the toe) Now how much fun would that be, Harrison . . . I bet that ant feels like he is on a ride at an amusement park like the one we went to last month." [Relating new to known]

Harrison: (Laughing) "I hope he doesn't fall off. . . . He looks scared like I was on that swing." [Relating new to known; active reading]

Kathy: "He does look scared. Do you remember the next animal?" [Encouraging predicting]

Harrison: "A lion! (Turning the page) . . . it's a dog!" [Disconfirming the prediction]

Kathy: "That's right . . . a dog. I WONDER WHAT IT WOULD BE LIKE TO BE A **DOG**." (Pointing to the illustration of the dog)

(Next page) "SNIFFING SO **WELL**, I COULD FIND THE SMALLEST CRUMB (with emphasis) **THAT FELL!**" (Pointing to the illustration of the crumb)

Kathy: (Turning the page) "I WONDER WHAT IT WOULD BE LIKE TO BE A **KANGAROO**." (With emphasis to remind Harrison of this animal)

(Next page) "JUMPING SO **HIGH**, I COULD REACH THE BLUE . . . (Pausing and pointing to the sky; encouraging predicting) **SKY**! Harrison do you remember when you were hopping around the room like a kangaroo?" [Relating new to known; monitoring understanding/active reading] (Harrison nods, and starts hopping around again)

(Harrison comes back and turns the page)

Kathy: "I WONDER WHAT IT WOULD BE LIKE TO BE A **LLLL** . . . **ION**! **R-o-a-r**! [Encouraging prediction, connecting letters/sounds/words with context] I remember I was wondering when we were looking at this picture before why that lion was in front of the crowd in this picture. Maybe he is performing at a circus . . . let's read and find out."

(Next page) "ROARING SO **LOUD** (raising voice), I COULD **SHHHH** (putting finger on lips and whispering) QUIET THE LARGEST CHEERING . . . [pausing and pointing to the crowd; encouraging predicting) **CROWD**!

Oh, this lion **was** trying to quiet the audience . . . maybe he does want to perform for them but he needs their attention." [Predicting-confirming/disconfirming; monitoring understanding]

Harrison: "Yeah, my dad took me to the circus and it was really noisy! There were lions and elephants, and it smelled!" (Harrison and Kathy start laughing) [Relating new to known, monitoring understanding]

Kathy: "Yes, there are a lot of people at circuses, and those elephants do stink sometimes, peehew!" [Responding to Harrison relating new to known]

Kathy: (Turning the page) "I WONDER WHAT IT WOULD BE LIKE TO BE A . . . " (Pointing to the illustration of the giraffe that is so tall its head is off the page) [Encouraging predicting]

Harrison "GIRAFFE!"

Kathy: (Pointing to the word giraffe) "Yes, GIRAFFE! [Confirming prediction; connecting letters/sounds/words with context]

(Next page) "STANDING SO **TALL** (With emphasis), I COULD BEAT MY BIG BROTHER IN . . . (Pausing and pointing to the illustration) **BASKET** . . . (pausing again) BAAA . . . " (Now pointing to the end part of the word basketball)

Harrison: "BALL!" [Predicting; connecting letters/sounds/words with context]

Kathy: "**Yes!** You read it! (Pointing again to the word) BASKETBALL!" (And then pointing back at the illustration) [Confirming Harrison's prediction; connecting letters/sounds/words with the context]

Harrison: "I can beat Jones (Harrison's brother) in basketball. I'm taller than him, but I can jump really high too." [Relating new to known; monitoring comprehension/active reading]

Kathy: "Yes, you are like a giraffe and a kangaroo." [Encouraging Harrison's reading behavior to relate new to known, monitoring comprehension/active reading]

Kathy: (Turning the page) "I WONDER WHAT IT WOULD BE LIKE TO BE A **PORCUPINE!** (Emphasizing and pointing to the porcupine) Remember I told you porcupines have needles called quills on their bodies like pine trees? Do you remember what they are like?" [Relating new to known]

Harrison: "Yeah, they are pointy." (Viewing next page)

Kathy: "FEELING SO **PRICKLY** (Poking Harrison all over his body with her finger), I COULD CHASE ENEMIES. . . . **QUI** . . . **QUI** . . . **QUICKLY!** [Connecting letters/sounds/words with context; encouraging prediction] I like how those words sound . . . **prickly** and **quickly**. They rhyme, don't they . . . prickly, quickly . . . and there's **sickly**, and **tickly**. (Tickles Harrison . . . he starts laughing) [Connecting letters/sounds/words with context] I don't think those quills would tickle, do you?" [Monitoring understanding/active reading]

Harrison: "Noooo . . . they would hurt."

Kathy: "I bet the meanest robber would run away."

Harrison: "Me too! No one would ever fight a porcupine!"

Kathy: "Very true." (Turning the page) I WONDER WHAT IT WOULD LIKE TO BE AN . . . (Pausing and pointing to illustration; predicting)

Harrison: "**ELEPHANT!**"

Kathy: (Pointing to the word) "That's right! **ELEPHANT**. You read the word!" [Confirming the prediction; connecting letters/sounds/words with context]

(Next page) "CREATED SO **LARGE**, I COULD SINK A FREIGHT . . .

Harrison, do you remember what you call this kind of boat?"

Harrison: (Shakes his head no)

Kathy: "It rhymes with large . . . b . . . bar . . . large . . . bar . . . .arge . . . **barge!**"

Harrison: (smiles)

Kathy: "Can you say **large** . . . **barge**?"

Harrison: "Large . . . barge."

Kathy: "That's right. (In a sing-song manner) Large . . . barge. Large . . . barge . . . (Harrison joins in) Large . . . barge. These words rhyme like before **prickly** . . . **quickly**. And **loud** . . . **crowd**. Can you hear the rhyme?" [Connecting letters/sounds/words with context]

Harrison: (Shakes his head yes)

Kathy: "Can you turn the page? (Harrison turns the page)

I WONDER WHAT IT WOULD BE LIKE TO BE A . . . " (Pausing and pointing to the illustration to encourage predicting)

Harrison: "**FOX!**"

Kathy: "That's right! You read the word!" (Pointing to the word to confirm the prediction)

(Next page) ACTING SO **SHYLY**, I COULD FRIEND A MOUSE . . . (pausing) sl...sl...

SLYLY! Shyly . . . **slyly**. That rhymes too! [Connecting letters/sounds/words with context]

This is an interesting picture . . . what does the fox have behind his back?" [Monitoring understanding]

Harrison: "A fork."

Kathy: "That's right . . . I wonder why he has that fork behind his back. . . . Looks like he is hiding it so the mouse can't see it. . . ." [Monitoring understanding]

Harrison: "I don't know."

Kathy: "Hmmm. Let's stop and think about this . . . What do we do with a fork?" [Monitoring understanding]

Harrison: "We eat food."

Kathy: "Yes, I'm thinking that foxes are very sly, which means they can trick you easily. Who might the fox want to eat?" [Monitoring understanding]

Harrison: "**The mouse!!!**"

Kathy: "Yes, the fox is so sly; he can make that mouse think he is his friend, when the fox really wants the mouse for dinner!" [Monitoring understanding]

Harrison: "That mouse is in **BIG** trouble."

Kathy: "He sure is . . . poor mouse." (Smiling)

Harrison: (Laughing and turning the page)

Kathy: "I WONDER WHAT IT WOULD BE LIKE TO BE A . . ." (Pausing and pointing to the illustration to encourage predicting)

Harrison: "**Lightning bug.**"

Kathy: "Yes, lightning bug." [Confirming the prediction—Although the text stated "firefly," this wasn't corrected because a firefly and lightning bug are the same. It will not change the meaning of the text]

(Next page) SHINING SO **BRIGHTLY**, I COULD LIGHT THE WORLD. . . . [Pausing and pointing to the word] . . . NNNNN . . . NNIII . . . Harrison, when do lightning bugs come out?"

Harrison: "At night."

Kathy: "That's right. SHINING SO BRIGHTLY, I COULD LIGHT THE WORLD NIGHT??? (Voice goes up) That doesn't sound exactly right. [Connecting letters/sounds/words with context; self-monitoring] SHINING SO BRIGHTLY, I COULD LIGHT THE WORLD NIGHT . . . LY! (Pausing for a few seconds)

That makes sense and sounds right, doesn't it? **Brightly** . . . **nightly** . . . rhymes too. Can you say that?" [Connecting letters/sounds/words with context]

Harrison: "Yeah. Brightly . . . nightly."

Kathy: "Very good. Can you imagine being able to light up the whole world like a huge light bulb?" [Relating new to known; self-monitoring for understanding]

Harrison: "No, I'd have to be really big! Bigger than that bulb." (Pointing to the light on the ceiling)

Kathy: "Yes, you would. (Laughing and then turning the page) MY HEAD IS A WORLD OF WONDER. IT SETS ME **FREE**.

(Next page) BUT I'M STILL GLAD I GET TO BE . . . (Pausing and pointing to the boy to encourage predicting) **ME**!

I guess the boy is smiling at the end because he would rather be himself than any of these other living things. Remember before we read, when we were just looking at the pictures, I thought maybe he was smiling because he had a good imagination; I was wrong; he does have a good imagination, too, but he just wants to be himself and not these other creatures!" [Disconfirming original prediction; monitoring understanding]

Harrison: (Shakes his head yes and smiles)

Let us stop here in the transcript because the next part is actually our final action stage, and that is **CONCLUDE** the shared book reading event.

LET'S REVIEW

So what are the most important points to remember about this chapter? First, parents are the mediators/facilitators who must explicitly demonstrate proficient reading behaviors during the shared book reading as they interact with their children. So your behaviors need to be contagious! You must show your enthusiasm for the reading as you engage in the four actions: 1) *Confirm and Make New Predictions* about what is going to happen in the text, 2) *Relate New Ideas to Known* as you connect with what might be personally significant to you and your child as you are reading, 3) *Connect Letters/Sounds/Words to Context and Illustrations* as you demonstrate print-based behaviors and (4) *Monitor* your and your child's *understanding* during active reading as you engage in think-alouds.

Second, this is by no means an exact science. And in fact, memorizing specific sample behaviors provided and modeled in the transcript is not the goal. Instead, the actions modeled should be viewed as examples of what might be done based on the text, personal experiences, and what the reader believes is most appropriate as it relates to the child's age, interest, and developmental level at that moment in time. You, as parents, track your children's abilities (that is, their *zone of proximal development*).

Third, you do not need an early childhood literacy degree to do this. If you try one of these *during reading* behaviors, and your child does not get it, then take a step back. Think about how you could make it a little bit easier the next time and model this behavior over and over again. Remember from chapter 1, you are always releasing more and more responsibility over to your children as they grow into literate human beings. Sometimes you will be on target as you scaffold and move them forward, and sometimes, you might need to take a step or two back if you see they are struggling.

So please do not view your shared book reading as *right* or *wrong*. Instead, treat every book reading experience as a way to hone your mediating behaviors as you facilitate your child's development. Most importantly, if the reading was pleasurable for both you and your child, you have been successful!

Chapter Eight

CONCLUDE: Don't Just Go to Sleep—Savor the Moment!

A conclusion brings any activity to a finish, which makes sense because we would not want any event to go on and on forever; humans want closure. Conclusions should allow us to think about major ideas in personal ways, ponder broader issues, and appreciate the topics and/or activity presented. Yet, not all conclusions are created equally. Case in point:

One evening when visiting a friend, a mom was invited to sit in on her friend Jessica's daughter's bedtime reading routine. Jessica and her daughter had been engaging in a wonderfully pleasurable reading of a fairytale, laughing and interacting throughout the reading. But the ending of the storybook read-aloud went something like this—"And they never wanted for anything ever again. . . . The END!" Jessica then abruptly slammed the book closed, kissed her daughter on the forehead, turned off the light, and left the room. Stunned by the very curt ending to a loving mother-daughter moment, it was only seconds before her daughter started crying, which soon turned into a roaring scream! Now one might argue that it was the darkness that made little Kelsey cry LOUDLY, but it seems that it was at least partly due to not bringing the ending of this wonderful shared book reading to a satisfying closure.

Any shared book reading should be celebrated, even if it is for just a few minutes. See figure 8.1 for the four **CONCLUDE** actions introduced in chapter 5.

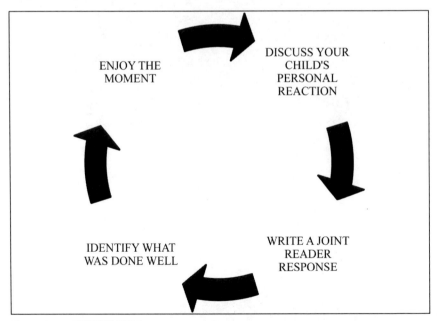

Figure 8.1.   CONCLUDE Stage

As with the *before reading* and the *during reading* stages, *after reading* actions overlap and are continuous, not sequential, and there is no requirement to complete each one every time you read.

DISCUSS YOUR CHILD'S PERSONAL REACTION

After you finish reading the book, please don't close the book with a *"The End!"* because you are not only closing the book, but shutting down your children's thinking, as well as enjoyment. Instead, a response to the reading is in order, which lends itself to the first *after reading* action—*Discuss Your Child's Personal Reaction.* This is quite simply a time when you explicitly and implicitly nurture your child's thinking by reflecting on what was just read.

As children's literacy develops, parents should be guiding them to be critical thinkers. So a reaction to the book is not just a recall of what the child understood, but instead it involves how certain parts of the book impressed the child in some way. Since all children and adults bring their personal experiences to every reading event, every response is unique because we are all individuals. There are no right or wrong answers.

How do you facilitate this? You begin through conversation as you model your own thinking and natural questioning. For example, assuming a parent had just completed reading the *All about Preschool* book, the parent might demonstrate a *personal reaction* by focusing on examples of the teacher's kindness throughout the book. A mother's response might be "I loved how Ms. Whitestone was thoughtful. She hugged one little girl when she missed her dad, and when the little boy scraped his knee, Ms. Whitestone quickly brought him to the nurse for a Band-Aid."

Since the books you are reading to your children have illustrations, which are crucial to the construction of meaning for emerging readers, it is important to engage in picture *look-backs* along with these reactions. So it would be effective for this mother to flip back and look at the illustrations that matched the kind teaching behaviors on which she just focused (hugging and bringing the child to the nurse).

After a brief discussion of those illustrations, the mother might then hand the book to her daughter and say, "This was my favorite part. What part of the book did you like best?" This will foster not only recall of the story but also nurture the child's critical thinking. So, first demonstrate the behavior for your child, and then try to nudge your child to try it out himself or herself. It is okay if children have some difficulty with this task, and it should be expected; this is when parents jump in and assist in finding a page that stands out for the youngster. The illustrations will make it easier for the child to respond to the book, and for younger children, it might be more appropriate for him or her just to find an illustration he or she liked. All behaviors can be modified to best *fit* your child.

This reader response activity with your children should be as natural as any other conversations you have with them; however, below is a list of prompts that might facilitate this natural dialogue, and the list usually tugs on personal emotions, interests, experiences, and points of view. Remember, the level of your prompts and interaction will become more sophisticated as your child's literacy knowledge develops.

- I loved this illustration because _____. Which picture did you like best?
- I enjoyed this part of the story _____. What part of the story did you like best?
- Can you find the page where _____ happened?
- I was surprised when _____. Here it is on this page; do you remember this?
- I thought this part was very sad because _____.
- Which person in the story did you like best? Why did you like him or her?
- Which animal (object, tool, insect, etc.) did you like best? Why?
- This part reminded me of when we_____.
- This person reminded me of (someone you both know) _____.
- Would you ever like to be (character or animal in the story) _____?
- This part was very silly. It made me laugh!
- From reading this book, I learned (state a new fact you learned) _____. What did you learn?
- I didn't like this part of the book because _____.
- I didn't enjoy this book because _____.

The possibilities of your *after reading* reactions are endless, and once again the reading event is unique based on the parent and child engaging in the shared book reading.

WRITE A JOINT READER RESPONSE

Let us take this one step further and make a reading-writing connection. Responding to reading through dialogue with your child is certainly a positive way to end the shared book reading; however, integrating a writing activity is also a natural way to demonstrate to young children that reading and writing are linked to one another. This can easily be accomplished through the second *after reading* activity, that is, *Writing a Joint Reader Response.* Writing? Young children don't write, do they?

Sure they do. Writing is a thinking activity. It is goal oriented and purposeful. Just observe preschoolers for a few minutes and you will see that they are purposeful beings with strong thoughts! Just as you act as mediators of your children's reading when you read aloud to them until they have mastered the ability to decode, you can also mediate a written response to any reading. Until your child learns how to write, you can ask him or her to dictate and then you can write what he or she says. As stated before, reader reactions are personal; no two responses will be identical, and there is an importance that children feel when they see their own thoughts, their words, down on paper.

So why not try writing with your children one day after you read with them. Buy a notebook, any type will do, but marble notebooks are very durable, and follow these simple steps:

1. Tell (or remind) your children that the reading log is a special notebook for writing down their thoughts about books you have read together, and you will write the words for them. You will also write down what you are thinking.
2. Write the title of the book you just read at the top (and date). Read the title of the book to your children as you point to the title.
3. Provide a prompt. Any prompt that was listed from the first *after reading* action will work, but you can come up with your own. Record your response.
4. Invite your children to do the same. Write down whatever they dictate to you. (Try to avoid corrections!)
5. Ask if they can think of anything else they want to say.
6. Review what was written by reading what you both wrote; follow along with your finger in a sweeping motion.
7. Ask your children if they would like to draw a picture to go along with the words. (For very young children, a drawing, and perhaps labeling the drawing under it, will be enough.)

So, the mother's reader response about the kind teacher described previously can easily be extended into a written reader response. Using the reader response log, the mother now might write:

"All about Preschool   September 5, 2012
'I liked the teacher in this book. She was kind because she helped the little girl feel better when she missed her daddy.'"

(The mother is saying the words as she writes the words.)

The mother then might ask her daughter, "What did you like about the teacher in this book?" (This is the prompt.) As the child responds (dictates) her thoughts, the mother writes in the reader response log:

"I liked that the teacher sings a lot and plays the piano."

(The mother repeats her daughter's words as she writes this sentence in the log.)

Now the mother reads the log entry again as she follows along with her finger in a fluent fashion. If the child is interested in this activity, the mother then might invite her daughter to draw a picture about what they just wrote; this might be the perfect ending to this reading.

IDENTIFY WHAT WAS DONE WELL

"Great job!" "Nicely done!" As parents act as mediators of their children's reading, it is important to praise children for their efforts. Have you ever noticed though, that the most effective coaches, teachers, and trainers point out specifics of what was done well with their tenderfoots? Children need to be made aware of the literacy behaviors they engaged in until this knowledge has been internalized, and they become aware of it themselves without your help. *Identifying What Was Done Well* is the third **CONCLUDE** action. It is an explicit action; parents' comments should be unambiguous.

During this action, a parent might bring to the forefront a behavior the child engaged in before, during, or after the shared book reading. If you recall from Cambourne's Model of Learning in chapter 1, timely feedback from parents is crucial. To get a better idea of what is meant by specific feedback, an assortment of comments parents can make have been listed:

- I liked how you used the title of the book and the picture on the cover to make a great prediction about what this book will be about. This is what good readers do.
- I liked how you told me that one of these pictures in this book was very much like another book we read the other day. This is what good readers do.
- I liked how you found the beginning of the book. This is what good readers do.
- I liked how you turned the pages as you followed along. This is what good readers do.
- I liked how you looked at the pictures as we read to help you understand the story. This is what good readers do.

- I liked how you were able to find the color words (or any other words) I was reading to you because you know their beginning sounds. This is what good readers do.
- I liked how you are following along with me as I read the words to you. This is what good readers do.
- I liked how you stopped me when you didn't understand what I was reading. This is what good readers do.
- I liked how you found your favorite part of the book after we read. This is what good readers do.
- I liked how you drew the most important part in the story. This is what good readers do.
- I like how you saw that my favorite part and your favorite part were different. This is what good readers do.
- I liked how you drew something you learned in the book. This is what good readers do.
- I liked how you noticed that the end of this book was very much like what happened to us the other day. This is what good readers do.
- I liked how you reread what we wrote in our reading logs. This is what good readers do.

This list could go on, but do you get the idea? Basically, what you are trying to accomplish is to make children aware of the specific reading actions during the **PREP, ENGAGE**, and **CONCLUDE** stages as well as what was learned about language and reading in the beginning chapters. How do you know what to say as far as your feedback? It all depends on your children's actions, but most importantly, be as explicit as possible. It is a reminder to your children of what they are doing well until they can remind themselves!

ENJOY THE MOMENT

While many might consider reading a book an individual activity, shared book readings with your children are social events where adults and children listen, talk, read, and play together. This social event should be celebrated, or in other words, it is our final **CONCLUDE** action, *Enjoy the Moment.* Your disposition, or emotional outlook, toward your shared book reading is most apparent as you bring the shared book reading event to a conclusion, and this will have a tremendous impact on your children's developing identities as readers. What value do you give to the shared book reading event? How do your actions define the reading—as a privilege or a job? Is the event rushed or savored?

Herbert Blumer (1969) wrote that humans act toward things based on the meanings these things have for them, and these individual meanings come from the social interactions one has with others. Therefore, through interaction, you will bring meaning to how your children define a shared book reading event, and your behaviors will nudge them toward developing positive dispositions or negative dispositions as readers. All book reading events should end with feelings of *privilege* and *pleasure*; this will motivate your children to want to do this again and again.

So celebrate! This doesn't mean that every time you finish reading a book with your child, a band should come marching in with a bunch of balloons. A celebration can be as simple as marking the shared book reading event as pleasurable ("This was such a great book; I'm so glad we were able to share it together!"), to perhaps acknowledging the shared book reading event later to other family members over dinner ("Today, Orlando and I read this great book together, and he would like to tell you about it.").

Once in a while, a more formal literacy celebration is more fitting. Perhaps this could take place after a certain number of books have been read, or something new has been learned, or the reading log is now full of thoughts. These special *Literacy Celebration* days (or nights) are times when your children are made to feel special for all they have accomplished as literate beings. During these more formal celebrations, food is always a plus. What's a celebration without food? So pizza night, or baking cookies, or a cake, would all work great.

Also, invite some guests, whether it is siblings, cousins, grandparents, friends, or whoever. Stuffed animals are great guests, too; they always enjoy a party! Let these be times when your children can share some of the many books they have read (perhaps with a reading log as a prop, or what is termed a *literacy artifact*), discuss why they liked or disliked these books, and talk about what they have learned.

You could also plan a *Literacy Date*, rather than a play date, with other parents you are friendly with who also enjoy reading with their young children. This is a great way to share experiences with parents about how they read to their children as well as share and borrow children's books from each other. Most importantly, it will bring respect and enjoyment to the socially created event as your youngsters will view themselves as readers. Try it—it is much more fun than just playing. Your children will love it!

ACTION!

One last time, let us step back into the shared book reading with Harrison and observe **CONCLUDE** behaviors in action. If you recall from the last chapter, the reading of *A Wondrous World in My Head* ended by first clarifying why the little boy is smiling in the illustration. ("He would rather be himself than any of these other living things.") Then a connection with the book ending was made with the prediction before reading. ("I thought maybe he was smiling because he had a good imagination.") However, instruction didn't stop there, but instead there was a follow-up statement disconfirming the prediction. ("I was incorrect; he does have a good imagination, too, but he just wants to be himself and not these other living things!") Below are the final minutes of this pleasurable shared book reading event with Harrison:

Kathy: (With the book still open to the smiling boy page) "This was such a great book to read!" [Demonstrating a positive disposition toward the reading]

(Turning to the page of the kangaroo in the clouds) I think my favorite part of this book was when the boy imagined he was a kangaroo. I think it would be so much fun to be able to jump so high that I could see over all of the houses on our street. I could look into the backyards in the summer and see what everyone was doing. [Reader response]

Harrison, did you like this part?"

Harrison: (Shaking his head yes)

Kathy: (Handing the book over to Harrison) "Can you find a page you liked?" [Encouraging a reader response]

Harrison: (Turning the pages and then stopping at the giraffe playing basketball) "I like this page. (Points to the illustration) I have a basket at home, and I play with my brother and my dad. I would like to be as tall as a giraffe and beat my dad. (He giggles) I could always get the ball in (as he stretches his arms all the way up and acts like he is shooting the basketball). That would be GREAT!"

Kathy: "That would be great. If I was the kangaroo and you were the giraffe, we could both get the ball in. We would make a great team! (Demonstrating this with her arms) I could reach the basket by jumping high, and you could just walk over to the basket and drop it in." [Encouraging further conversation related to Harrison's response to the reading]

(They both smile)

Kathy: (Taking out the reader response log) "Harrison, do you remember what we have been using this for?"

Harrison: (Shakes his head yes) "Yeah, we write in it."

Kathy: "That's right. And draw, too. I was thinking today maybe we could think of some other animals we might like to be and write a sentence about it, and maybe draw a picture. Would you like to do this?" [Writing a joint reader response]

Harrison: (Shakes his head yes)

Kathy: "Let's think. What might be a fun animal? Hmmmm."

(Wait time is provided)

Harrison: "I like bears. (Pauses) No, how about a monkey!" (Starts jumping around like a monkey)

Kathy: "That is a wonderful choice. How about I write the sentence and you draw the picture."

Harrison: "Okay."

Kathy: (Saying the words slowly and writing the words) "I - wonder - what - it - would - be - like - to - be - a - monkey." (Passing the notebook to Harrison)

Harrison: (Takes a brown crayon and starts drawing a monkey) "I like monkeys because they can swing in trees." (I get some cookies for us to eat while he is drawing) [Writing a joint reader response; enjoying the moment—celebrating literacy]

Kathy: "I'd love to swing from tree to tree. They are good climbers too."

Harrison: (Continuing to draw) "I'm a good climber! I can climb that tree in my backyard."

Kathy: "You are just like a monkey!"

Harrison: (Smiling and as he finishes the drawing he passes the notebook to me) "There, I'm done."

Kathy: "I love your monkey. Let's read the sentence again together."

Kathy and Harrison: (Kathy reads the sentence slowly and points to the words in a sweeping motion as Harrison whispers a few of the words from memory) "I wonder what it would be like to be a . . . (Pausing) monkey!" (They both shout together) [Writing a joint reader response]

Kathy: "Harrison, it was so much fun to read with you today. When we were reading, I liked how you were able to guess the next word I was about to read by looking at the picture. Remember when we were looking at this page (turning to the illustration of the elephant). You guessed elephant! And you did it again on this page. (Turning to the page with the illustration of the firefly) You guessed lightning bug. This is what good readers do. They make guesses." [Identifying what was done well]

(Harrison's dad walks into the house)

Kathy: "Kevin, can you come here. Harrison and I just read a great book called *A Wondrous World in My Head* and maybe he can show the book to you." [Enjoying the moment by celebrating with his dad]

Kevin: "Hi Harrison. Wow, let me see."

Kathy: "Harrison, can you show your dad your favorite part?" [Enjoying the moment; discuss your child's personal reaction]

Harrison: (Taking the book) "Daddy, I liked this picture because the giraffe is so tall. I wanted to be the giraffe so I could beat you in basketball!"

Kevin: (Laughing) "Harrison, the way you are growing, before you know it, you will be as tall as that giraffe! I love this picture."

Kathy: "Harrison also thought it would be fun to be a monkey. See his picture." (Pointing to the written response and picture in the reader response log) [Enjoying the moment]

Kevin: "Harrison, you drew that? You are a great artist, and I also think you are a monkey sometimes. You climb on everything." (Picking his son up in the air)

Harrison: (Giving his dad a cookie, and starting to lose interest now in the book)

Kathy: "Harrison, I had such a great time reading with you today. I hope we can do it again soon. Maybe you can take this book home with you and read it again with your mom or dad."

Kevin: "That's a great idea!"

Harrison: (Smiling, picks the book up and another part of his daily routine begins)

LET'S REVIEW

This is just one demonstration that included several actions that can occur after the shared book reading event. Notice how each action is integrated into what is naturally occurring, but the adult reader acts to guide the *after reading* process based on the clues the child is giving throughout the interaction. Tune in to clues your children are giving. They will be your road map. This means—be an **active** observer of your children's responses as you engage in this *after reading* interaction!

Remember, the level and sophistication of your *after reading* actions will depend on the age/developmental level of your child. How will you know this? By trial and error. Try an action, and if it is unsuccessful, take a step back and try an easier action. *Discussing Your Child's Personal Reaction* can be brief and simple, like asking your child to find his or her favorite page or draw a favorite part of the book.

As your child becomes more comfortable with this, you can begin to raise your expectations and try the more sophisticated reader responses like stating what you learned and following up by asking your child what he or she learned from reading this book. Scaffolding onto this might be to list all the things you both learned from reading the book as you *Write a Joint Reader Response*. If your child is not "getting" this, then model this action, and the next time you read, make it a slightly easier task.

Remember, being a good observer or *kid watcher* means *Identifying What Was Done Well*, but also knowing when to stop! The shared *after reading* scenario presented in this chapter included interaction at its best, so it was easy to find specific reading behaviors to praise. But sometimes the *after reading* is just not enjoyable, not because it is not at the right developmental level, but due to some other reason. It could be because it was a poor choice of book and the child was not connecting with the illustrations, topics, or author's style of writing. Or perhaps the youngster enjoyed the book but is now just tired or more interested in doing something else at that point in the day. This is okay; it is just time to end the *after reading* activity. (Also, if a child is truly not enjoying a book at the *during reading* stage, a parent should abandon it and make a different book choice.)

Don't force the process. We are always looking for positive experiences, and if this isn't occurring, it can be harmful to the child's reading disposition, that is, how they feel and act toward reading. Remember a successful shared book reading event is always viewed as pleasurable and not a chore! Your ultimate goal is to *Enjoy the Moment.*

FINAL THOUGHTS

Chapter Nine

From the Womb to the Kindergarten Classroom!

For all we know about teaching and learning, there often still seems to be a general undervaluing of the highly qualified early-childhood teacher. Yet, every interaction, activity, and project conducted in an early-childhood setting is critical to the language and literacy development of those children.

Case in point:

Recently, while having dinner at a local Italian restaurant with a childhood friend, one of her preschoolers came up to our table and said, "Hi, Ms. B. Look, I'm reading the menu just like in school!" As the preschooler opened the menu she proudly carried, she began to pretend read her favorites: "spaghetti, pizza, meatballs, fettacheezee. . . ." My friend smiled at the little girl and complimented her fine reading and how much she had learned.

After the child left, my friend modestly explained that she and her students had been playing restaurant in her classroom. She then followed up with "I can't believe I ended up as just a preschool teacher . . . I feel so insignificant." Surprised by her comment, a long conversation ensued about the essential work she did every day for the past twenty years with her preschoolers, and how she was making a lifetime difference with each child she touched. Her authentic approach to literacy development was making a world of difference for every child.

Noting a bit of research, we see that Block, Oakar, and Hurt (2002) argued that student literacy development on all levels often depends on teacher expertise for instruction, classroom context, and the actions taken by their teacher (e.g., caring about and advocating for students, responsive teaching, and individualized instruction). Early childhood education teachers must be knowledgeable in the areas of language acquisition, second-language learning, the reading and writing processes, and early literacy development as well as have obtained many practice hours in order to develop their instructional expertise (NAEYC and IRA 1998). In short, the quality of the preschool is based on accomplished teachers.

ALL PRESCHOOLS ARE NOT CREATED EQUALLY

So while this book has focused on the very important and critical role of you, the parents, in developing your children's literacy, early childhood teachers also strongly impact your children's literacy identities. It is therefore also important to spend at least some brief time discussing how to select the *right* preschool for your children.

There is tons of research to support the idea that the early years, from birth to the age of eight, are crucial to later school success as well as in life. Appropriate early language and literacy experiences are a must for *all* children because they foster future academic success in the elementary grades, high school, and beyond (Barnett 1995; Cunningham and Stanovich 1997; Dickinson, McCabe, and Essex 2006; Ramey and Ramey 2006). Literacy learning is an ongoing process that begins in the earliest of years; children do not go from the womb to the kindergarten classroom. This being the case, it is not a great leap to state that "Preschools make a difference. . . . High-quality preschools embrace appropriate early literacy experiences delivered by well-prepared, knowledgeable, caring preschool teachers*"* (International Reading Association 2005, p. 1).

In 1998, two renowned education organizations, the National Association for the Education of Young Children (NAEYC) and the International Reading Association (IRA) stood together and published a position statement, "Learning to Read and Write: Developmentally Appropriate Practices for Young Children." These organizations believed this statement would "contribute significantly to an improvement in practice and the development of supportive educational policies" (p. 4) and would provide guidance to early childhood educators, administrators, and policy makers. In short, the NAEYC and the IRA recommended policies to ensure early childhood programs provide developmentally appropriate literacy experiences for all children. These recommendations are on target; however, many preschools have not put these policies into practice still today!

These recommendations are excellent criteria for parents when they are selecting preschools for their children. Therefore, below is a list of guided questions you can ask when exploring potential preschools; they are based on the 1998 NAEYC and IRA recommendations. Following each question, there is a brief statement explaining *why* the question is so important to ask.

1. How qualified are the teachers who are hired? What is their level of education and have they completed college degrees in early childhood education and/or literacy education? In order to be effective, early-childhood-education teachers must be knowledgeable of language acquisition, second-language learning, and early reading and writing development. Surprisingly, in the United States there are no uniform preparation requirements or licensure standards for teachers of children younger than kindergarten. So while some preschool teachers hold master's degrees in education, other preschool

teachers may not have completed an undergraduate degree in education. Some only hold high school diplomas.

2. Are the hired teachers required to participate in ongoing professional development? It is mandatory for K–12 teachers to continue their professional preparation, but this is not true for preschool teachers. For preschools, the level of ongoing professional development required is vague and based on the decisions of the individual preschool administration; thus, it is inconsistent from preschool to preschool. The world is constantly changing and new knowledge always evolving. Preschool teachers must stay current with new and innovative ways of teaching and learning standards.

3. What is the ratio of qualified teachers to children? Research shows that young children learn best in small-group settings. Developmental levels of children will always vary; in order for preschool teachers to be able to identify and provide differentiated instruction, they need small class size.

4. How do the teachers assess their preschoolers' literacy development? Authentic assessments, such as observation with detailed anecdotal notes while children are completing daily reading and writing tasks, are highly recommended. Group testing should not be given to young children. It is often not valid and does not demonstrate the preschoolers' true developmental level.

5. If a child is not making continuous literacy progress, what types of resources are available to provide more individualized instruction? Are there any teachers holding literacy degrees? If a child is not making satisfactory progress in literacy, it is imperative that the school and parents work together to intervene as early as possible. This can only be done if there are teachers in the school who have a *knowing literacy eye* with a surplus of instructional strategies and recommendations for parents.

6. What types of high quality children's books (and ebooks) at various readability levels are available? Do the books reflect the culture and backgrounds of the students? Does the preschool have any connection with the public library? Preschool children should be surrounded by a wealth of relatable and appealing books. Classroom libraries are a must! Children become lifelong readers by being immersed in a world of interesting books; they should always be available and viewed as part of children's daily routines. Public libraries and preschools should communicate with each other in order to provide family support.

While surely you are not selecting a college, what happens with your children's education today will have an impact on their future academic success. In 2006, two experts in the field of early literacy education, Kathleen Roskos and Carol Vukelich, addressed early literacy policy and practice stating that there should be not only an urgency to teach young children to read and write competently in order to achieve the high standards of literacy necessary in today's society but also an equal urgency to develop, and expect the highest performance from, our preschool programs.

Preschool teachers are the *change strategy* for young children's literacy development. There is a strong need to increase the literacy development of young children, but this outcome cannot be achieved unless we begin to hire and *value* the highest quality preschool teachers. Until this is universal, parents need to be selective when deciding on their children's preschool education.

COLLEGE AND CAREER READY? MY CHILD IS JUST ENTERING KINDERGARTEN!

In 2013, a new set of standards in English Language Arts, led by the National Governors Association Center for Best Practices and the Council of Chief State School Officers, was implemented across the United States (forty-five states and the District of Columbia had already done so as of September 2012) for K–12 grades. They are called the Common Core State Standards (CCSS), which many parents may already be aware of since there has been some controversy in local and national news over their implementation.

The purpose of this educational reform is to ensure that all students are college and career ready by the time they complete high school. Specifically, these standards were written to equip teachers with a set of core conceptual understandings and procedures that will act as benchmarks for what students need to learn at every grade level. The CCSS are divided into strands: Reading, Writing, Speaking, Listening, and Language, each of which is followed by its standards. The Reading strand is congruent with the purpose of this book, and therefore the standards that will be addressed in this final chapter are from this strand.

For kindergarten, the English Language Arts Standards for Reading are divided into three areas: Literature, Informational Text, and Foundational Skills. Literature and Informational Text standards focus on exposing children to a wide range of texts, both fiction and nonfiction. Foundational Skills standards address students' knowledge of concepts of print, the alphabetic principle, and conventions of the English writing system. See table 9.1 for a chart of each specific standard that your children will be required to master by the end of kindergarten.

Table 9.1. Common Core State Standards for Reading—Kindergarten

Literature	Informational Text	Foundational Skills
• **Key Ideas and Details** • With prompting and support, ask and answer questions about key details in a text. • With prompting and support, retell familiar stories, including key details. • With prompting and support, identify characters, settings, and major events in a story.	• **Key Ideas and Details** • With prompting and support, ask and answer questions about key details in a text. • With prompting and support, identify the main topic and retell key details of a text. • With prompting and support, describe the connection between two individuals, events, ideas, or pieces of information in a text.	• **Print Concepts** • Demonstrate understanding of the organization and basic features of print. • Follow words from left to right, top to bottom, and page by page. • Recognize that spoken words are represented in written language by specific sequence of letters. • Understand that words are separated by spaces in print. • Recognize and name all upper- and lowercase letters of the alphabet.
• **Craft and Structure** • Ask and answer questions about unknown words in a text. • Recognize common types of texts (e.g., storybooks, poems). • With prompting and support, name the author and illustrator of a story and define the role of each in telling the story.	• **Craft and Structure** • With prompting and support, ask and answer questions about unknown words in a text. • Identify the front cover, back cover, and title page of a book. • With prompting and support, name the author and illustrator of a text and define the role of each in presenting the ideas or information in a text.	• **Phonological Awareness** • Demonstrate understanding of spoken words, syllables and sounds (phonemes). • Recognize and produce rhyming words. • Count, pronounce, blend, and segment syllables in spoken words. • Blend and segment onsets and rimes of single-syllable spoken words. • Isolate and pronounce the initial, medial vowel, and final sounds (phonemes) in three phoneme (consonant-vowel-consonant) words. • Add or substitute individual sounds (phoneme) in simple, one-syllable words to make new words.

Literature	Informational Text	Foundational Skills
• **Integration of Knowledge and Ideas** • With prompting and support, describe the relationship between illustrations and the story in which they appear. • With prompting and support, compare and contrast the adventures and experiences of characters in familiar stories.	• **Integration of Knowledge and Ideas** • With prompting and support, describe the relationship between illustrations and the text in which they appear (e.g., what person, place, thing, or idea in the text illustration depicts). • With prompting and support, identify the reasons an author gives to support points in a text. • With prompting and support, identify basic similarities in and differences between two texts on the same topic (e.g., illustrations, descriptions, or procedures).	• **Phonics and Word Recognition** • Know and apply grade-level phonics and word analysis skills in decoding words. • Demonstrate basic knowledge of one-to-one letter-sounds correspondences by producing the primary sound or many of the most frequent sounds for each consonant. • Associate the long and short sounds with the common spellings (graphemes) for the five major vowels. • Read common high-frequency words by sight (eg., the, of, to, you). • Distinguish between similarly spelled words by identifying the sounds of the letters that differ.
• **Range of Reading and Level of Text Complexity** • Actively engage in group reading activities with purpose and understanding.	• **Range of Reading and Level of Text Complexity** • Actively engage in group reading activities with purpose and understanding.	• **Fluency** • Read emergent-reader texts with purpose and understanding.

Source: The Common Core State Reading Standards by the National Governors Association Center for Best Practices and the Council of Chief State School Officers 2010.

As you familiarize yourself with each standard, try to begin formulating ways you might naturally foster these concepts and skills during your shared book reading event. Let us revisit the shared book reading activity with Harrison during the **ENGAGE** stage to demonstrate how easy this is to do; here is a portion of the transcript:

> Kathy: "I WONDER WHAT IT WOULD BE LIKE TO BE A **PORCUPINE**! (Emphasizing and pointing to the porcupine) Remember I told you porcupines have needles called quills on their bodies like pine trees? Do you remember what they are like?" [Relating new to known]
>
> Harrison: "Yeah, they are pointy." (Turns the page)
>
> Kathy: "FEELING SO **PRICKLY** (Poking Harrison all over his body with her finger), I COULD CHASE ENEMIES . . . **QUI** . . . **QUI** . . . **QUICKLY**! [Connecting letters/sounds/words with context; encouraging prediction] I like how those words sound . . . **prickly** and **quickly**. They rhyme, don't they . . . prickly, quickly . . . and there's **sickly**, and **tickly**. (Tickles Harrison . . . he starts laughing) [Connecting letters/sounds/words with context] I don't think those quills would tickle, do you?" [Monitoring understanding/active reading]
>
> Harrison: "Noooo . . . they would hurt."
>
> Kathy: "I bet the meanest robber would run away."
>
> Harrison: "Me too! No one would ever fight a porcupine!"

During this brief shared book reading snippet with Harrison, there are several Common Core State Standards highlighted:

- *Craft and Structure—With prompting and support, ask and answer questions about unknown words in a text.* Several words were discussed during this interaction, that is, *porcupine*, *quills*, and *prickly*.
- *Integration of Knowledge and Ideas: With prompting and support, describe the relationship between illustrations and the text in which they appear.* An illustration–text connection was made with the porcupine illustration and the words.
- *Foundational Skills—Phonological Awareness: Recognize and produce rhyming words.* Harrison is explicitly told how *prickly* and *quickly* rhyme, and then other words are added (*sickly* and *tickly*) to further Harrison's knowledge base about rhyming words.

This is just an example, but in fact all the kindergarten CCSS are consistent with the **PREP**, **ENGAGE**, and **CONCLUDE** actions introduced to you in this book. Are your children's kindergarten teachers responsible for achieving each of these standards? Yes. However, keep in mind that the more exposure your children have in practicing these tasks, the greater the chance the tasks will be overlearned and utilized independently. Additionally, as the National Association for the Education of Young Children (2012) recently pointed out, all kindergartens are expected to have the same learning outcomes, but kindergarten experiences across the United States vary in regard to curriculum as well as structurally (half and full day programs).

The Common Core State Standards are meant to act as a set of criteria to improve student learning and achievement. Rather than using scripted literacy programs, from the early years, it is worthwhile to create authentic environments that naturally foster the likelihood of achieving these learning outcomes (CCSS). This book can be used as way of naturally addressing many of these standards.

PARENTS ARE MOST IMPORTANT!

Parents, your children are becoming literate right before your very eyes! This is exciting to watch and is the responsibility of both your children's teachers and you. Let's return one last time to the notable cognitive psychologist Lev Vygotsky, who in 1978 wrote, "Children grow into the intellectual life around them." Your beliefs about reading and your knowledge about reading, influence your actions when you are reading with your children. These perceptions and understandings are *inherited* by your children.

Several recommendations have been provided for you to consider when selecting schools for your youngsters. However, ultimately, you are with your children from the first day they are born and the language you use, the atmosphere you create, and the actions you engage in influence your children's reading identities. By inviting your children to engage in effective reading behaviors during shared book reading, you are helping them develop characteristics of proficient readers.

The key is being consistent by engaging in these activities over and over again. Soon your children will begin to orchestrate these **PREP, ENGAGE,** and **CONCLUDE** stages on their own, and as exciting as it was to see them take their first steps, you will *catch* them stepping into conventional reading. Cheer them on as they continue to develop these behaviors during the first years of formal schooling.

Before this workshop ends, it is important to again mention that the focus when writing this book was on developing youngsters' *comprehension*. While both print-based and meaning-based behaviors were addressed, both important components of reading, the emphasis was purposely on understanding. All too often literacy educators have seen parents, and classroom teachers, focus solely on the child's ability to decode (for example, learning the alphabet with the accompanying sounds; identifying sight words), with the belief that comprehension will come naturally if the child can decode, but this is not the case. The construction of meaning is of utmost importance!

In the fall of 2010, a renowned literacy expert, Susan B. Neuman, wrote the article "Sparks Fade, Knowledge Stays: The National Early Literacy Panel's Report Lacks Staying Power." In this article, Neuman addressed which literacy practices have more *staying power*. What is most important for children to acquire in order to achieve in later years? According to Neuman, it is critical for children to develop the complex knowledge, skills, and strategies required for reading comprehension. The focus must be on building vocabulary and world knowledge. Young children are *natural knowledge seekers*, and parents, your goal is to facilitate this through shared book reading. These early literacy practices are the foundation for conventional reading.

No one ever said parenting would be easy, and certainly the responsibility you have been asked to consider in this book is the more difficult path. This book has guided you to be more knowledgeable of the thinking processes as well as the emotional aspects of reading in order to become more effective partners with your children during shared book reading. Be *mindful* of not only your children's physical health, but also, of their literacy health. By following the instructional plan presented in this book, you will help create your children's literacy *habit of mind* and a love for reading; this will foster their future academic success.

Preventative actions are always easier than intervention, and it is you who plays the greatest role in building your children's literacy identities. Guiding your children to understand the text and to personally connect to the author behind the words will make a world of difference. Remember, "Reading is not walking on the words; it's grasping the soul of them" (Freire 1985, 19).

Appendix A

A Wondrous World in My Head

My head is a world of wonder. It sets me free. There are so many living things I'd like to be!

I wonder what it would be like to
be an ant.

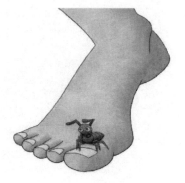

Crawling so low,
I could ride your big toe!

I wonder what it would be like to
be a dog.

Sniffing so well,
I could find the smallest crumb
that fell!

I wonder what it would be like to
be a kangaroo.

Jumping so high,
I could reach the blue sky!

I wonder what it would be like to
be a lion.

Roaring so loud,
I could quiet the largest cheering
crowd!

I wonder what it would be like to
be a giraffe.

Standing so tall,
I could beat my big brother in
basketball!

I wonder what it would be like to
be a porcupine.

Feeling so prickly,
I could chase enemies quickly!

I wonder what it would be like to be an elephant.

Created so large,
I could sink a freight barge!

I wonder what it would be like to be a fox.

Acting so shyly,
I could friend a mouse slyly!

I wonder what it would be like to
be a firefly.

Shining so brightly,
I could light the sky nightly!

My head is a world of wonder.
It sets me free.

But I'm still glad I get to be
ME!

Appendix B

Favorite Shared Book Reading List to Support Your Children's Literacy

Parents, while you and your children will enjoy exploring your library and bookstore for your favorite books, listed below are some of my suggestions. Several literacy educators who have a true passion for books have also graciously shared their favorite titles. Try a few—it is important, however, to read the books you select for shared reading before you read them to your child so you can decide if the book is *right* for your child. Foster a love of reading as you demonstrate to your children that books *amaze*, books *intrigue*, books *entertain*, books *teach*!

FOR INFANTS AND TODDLERS

Blue Hat, Green Hat by Sandra Boynton
Doggies by Sandra Boynton
The Going to Bed Book by Sandra Boynton
Goodnight Moon by Margaret Wise Brown
Goodnight, Goodnight Construction Site by Sherri Duskey Rinker
Time for Bed by Mem Fox
Animal Colors: Touch and Feel by Dorling Kindersley Publishing
Wild Animals: Touch and Feel by Dorling Kindersley Publishing
Good Morning, Good Night: A Touch and Feel Bedtime Book by Melanie Mitchell
Guess How Much I Love You by Sam McBratney
Lullaby Moon by Rosie Reeve
Pat the Bunny by Dorothy Kunhardt
Peek a Moo by Marie Torres Cimarusti
Tails by Matthew Van Fleet

FOR PRESCHOOLERS (AGES 3–5 AND BEYOND)

Storybooks and Information Books to Chant or Sing or Rhyme

Victor Vito and Freddie Vasco by Laurie Berkner
Big Red Barn by Margaret Wise Brown
Five Little Monkeys Jumping on the Bed by Eileen Christelow
Pete the Cat I Love My White Shoes by James Dean
Llama Llama Red Pajamas by Anna Dewdney
Ten Little Ladybugs by Melanie Gerth
Chicka Chicka Boom Boom by Bill Martin Jr. and John Archambault
Brown Bear, Brown Bear, What Do You See? by Bill Martin Jr. and Eric Carle
From Head to Toe by Eric Carle
My Truck Is Stuck by Kevin Lewis
The Book about Tony Chestnut by Laurie Monopoli
Down by the Bay by Raffi and Nadine Bernard Westcott
In the Garden by Elizabeth Spur
In the Woods by Elizabeth Spur
At the Beach by Elizabeth Spur
Fabulous Fishes by Susan Stockdale
Bring on the Birds by Susan Stockdale
Carry Me! Animal Babies on the Move by Susan Stockdale
Green Eggs and Ham by Dr. Seuss
The Cat in the Hat by Dr. Seuss
Sheep in a Jeep by Nancy Shaw
See You Later Alligator: A First Book of Rhyming Word-Play by Barbara Strauss and
    Helen Friedland
Has Anyone Seen My Green Dinosaur? by Lisa Trutkoff Trumbauer
Skip to My Lou by Nadine Bernard Westcott*A Million Chameleons* by James Young
The Wheels on the Bus by Paul O. Zelinsky

Additional Storybooks and Information Books

Blue Burt and Wiggles by Derek Anderson
The Spooky Old Tree by Stan and Jan Berenstain
The Mitten by Jan Brett
Clifford the Big Red Dog series by Norman Bridwell
Tarra and Bella: The Elephant and the Dog Who Became Best Friends by Carol
    Buckley
Mr. Gumpy's Outing by John Burningham
Snow Friends by Christina Butler
One Winter's Day by Christina Butler
Today is Monday by Eric Carle
The Very Hungry Caterpillar by Eric Carle
Duck by Randy Cecil

What Will I Be? (Lift the Flap Book) by Nicola Davies
Who Lives Here? (Lift the Flap Book) by Nicola Davies
Who's Like Me? (Lift the Flap Book) by Nicola Davies
Glad Monster, Sad Monster by Ed Emberley and Anne Miranda
Corduroy by Don Freeman
Wilfrid Gordon McDonald Partridge by Mem Fox
Zoo Looking by Mem Fox
Moonlight Ocean by Elizabeth Golding
Moonlight Animals by Elizabeth Golding
Little Toot by Hardy Gramatky
Shoo Scat by Lois G. Grambling
Spot Can Count by Eric Hill
The Doorbell Rang by Pat Hutchins
Peter's Chair by Ezra Jack Keats
The Snowy Day by Ezra Jack Keats
Leo the Late Bloomer by Robert Kraus
Little Blue and Little Yellow by Leo Lionni
Froggy series by Jonathon London
Blueberries for Sal by Robert McCloskey
The Cow That Went Oink by Bernard Most
If You Give a Mouse a Cookie by Laura Joffe Numeroff
The Lion and the Mouse (with audio) by Jerry Pinkney
Pattern by Henry (Concept Book) Pluckrose
Sorting by Henry (Concept Book) Pluckrose
Length by Henry (Concept Book) Pluckrose
Good Night Gorilla by Peggy Rathmann
Curious George series by H. A. Rey
Where The Wild Things Are by Maurice Sendak
Horton Hears a Who by Dr. Seuss
No, David by David Shannon
Caps for Sale by Ephyr Slobdkins
Kate and Pippin: An Unlikely Love Story by Martin Springett
Alexander and the Terrible, Horrible, No Good, Very Bad Day by Judith Viorst
Elephant and Piggie books by Mo Willems
Knuffle Bunny by Mo Willems
King Bidgoods in the Bathtub by Audrey Wood
Deep Sea Dive (Lift the Flap Book) by Salina Yoon
Space Walk (Lift the Flap Book) by Salina Yoon
Harry the Dirty Dog by Gene Zion
Harry by the Sea by Gene Zion
William's Doll by Charlotte Zolotow

References

Bandura, Albert. 1997. *Self-efficacy: The Exercise of Control.* New York: Freeman.

Barnett, W. Steven. 1995. "Long-Term Effects of Early Childhood Programs on Cognitive and School Outcomes." *The Future of Children* 5(3): 25–50.

Block, Cathy Collins, Margaret Oakar, and Nicholas Hurt. 2002. "The Expertise of Literacy Teachers: A Continuum from Preschool to Grade 5." *Reading Research Quarterly* 37(2): 178–206.

Bloom, Lois. 1970. *Language Development: Form and Function of Emerging Grammars.* Cambridge, MA: MIT Press.

Blumer, Herbert. 1969. *Symbolic Interactionism: Perspective and Method.* Englewood Cliffs, NJ: Prentice Hall.

Bruner, J. S. 1977. "Early Social Interaction and Language Development." In *Studies in Mother-Child Interaction,* edited by H. Rudolph Schaffer, 271–89. London: Academic Press.

Cambourne, Brian. 1988. *The Whole Story: Natural Learning and the Acquisition of Literacy in the Classroom.* New York: Ashton Scholastic.

Chomsky, Noam. 1968. *Language and Mind.* New York: Harcourt Brace Jovanovich.

Cunningham, Anne E., and Keith E. Stanovich. 1997. "Early Reading Acquisition and Its Relation to Reading Experience and Ability 10 Years Later." *Developmental Psychology* 33(6): 934–45.

Dickinson, David K., Allyssa McCabe, and Marilyn J. Essex. 2006. "A Window of Opportunity We Must Open to All: The Case for Preschool with High-quality Support for Language and Literacy." In *Handbook of Early Literacy Research Vol. 2,* edited by David K. Dickinson and Susan B. Neuman, 11–28. New York: The Guilford Press.

Dixon-Krauss, Lisbeth. 1996. *Vygotsky in the Classroom: Mediated Literacy Instruction and Assessment.* Upper Saddle River, NJ: Pearson.

Edmunds, Kathryn M., and Kathryn L. Bauserman. "What Teachers Can Learn about Reading Motivation through Conversations with Children." *The Reading Teacher* 59 (2006): 414–24.

Emerick, J. "The #1 Way to Melt Fat." *Self*, March, 2012.

Freire, Paulo. "Reading the World and Reading the Word: An Interview with Paulo Freire." *Language Arts* 62 (1985): 15–21.

Goetz, Ernest T., Diane L. Schallert, Ralph E. Reynolds, and Dean I. Radin. "Reading in Perspective: What Real Cops and Pretend Burglars Look for in a Story." *Journal of Educational Psychology* 75 (1983): 500–510.

Goldenberg, Claude. "Learning to Read in New Zealand: The Balance of Skills and Meaning." *Language Arts* 68 (1991): 555–62.

Goodman, Yetta M., and Carolyn Burke. 1980. *Reading Strategies: Focus on Comprehension.* New York: Richard C. Owen.

Hart, Betty, and Todd R. Risley. 1995. *Meaningful Differences in the Everyday Experiences of Young Children.* Baltimore: Brookes.

Huey, Edmund. B. 1908. *The Psychology and Pedagogy of Reading.* New York: MacMillan.

International Reading Association (IRA). 2005. *Literacy Development in the Preschool Years: A Position Statement.* Newark, DE: International Reading Association.

LaBerge, David, and S. Jay Samuels. "Toward a Theory of Automatic Information Processing in Reading." *Cognitive Psychology* 6 (1974): 293–323.

Moats, Louisa. Overcoming the Language Gap. *American Educator* Summer (2001): 5–9.

Morrow, Lesley Mandel, Jeanne Paratore, and Diane Tracey. 1994. *Family Literacy: New Perspectives, New Opportunities.* Newark, DE: International Reading Association.

National Association for the Education of Young Children (NAEYC) and International Reading Association (IRA). "NAEYC and IRA Joint Position Statement: Learning to Read and Write: Developmentally Appropriate Practices for Young Children." *Young Children* 53 (1998): 30–46.

National Governors Association Center for Best Practices and the Council of Chief State School Officers. 2010. *Common Core State Standards.* Washington D.C.: National Governors Association Center for Best Practices, Council of Chief State School Officers.

Neuman, Susan B. 2010. "Sparks Fade, Knowledge Stays." *American Educator* 34 (2010): 3.

Pajares, Frank. "Self-efficacy Beliefs, Motivation, and Achievement in Writing: A Review of the Literature." *Reading and Writing Quarterly* 19 (2003): 139–58.

Pearson, P. David, and Margaret C. Gallagher. "The Instruction of Reading Comprehension." *Contemporary Educational Psychology* 8 (1983): 317–44.

Piaget, Jean. 1957. *The Construction of Reality in the World.* London: Routledge.

Ramey, Sharon Landesman, and Craig T. Ramey. 2006. "Early Educational Interventions: Principles of Effective and Sustained Benefits from Targeted Early Education Programs." In *Handbook of Early Literacy Research, Vol. 2*, edited by David K. Dickinson and Susan B. Newman, 445–59. New York: The Guilford Press.

Rohlf, James W. 1994. *Modern Physics from α to Z⁰.* Hoboken, NJ: John Wiley & Sons.

Rosenblatt, Louise M. 1994. "The Transactional Theory of Reading and Writing." In *Theoretical Models and Processes of Reading,* 4th ed., edited by Robert B. Ruddell, Martha Rupp Ruddell, and Harry Singer, 1057–92. Newark, DE: International Reading Association.

Roskos, Kathleen, and Carol Vukelich. 2006. "Early Literacy Policy and Pedagogy." In *Handbook of Early Literacy Research, Vol. 2*, edited by David K. Dickinson and Susan B. Newman, 295–308. New York: Guilford.

Skinner, Burrhus Frederic. 1957. *Verbal Behavior.* New York: Appleton-Century-Crofts.

Smith, F. 2004. *Understanding Reading: A Psycholinguistic Analysis of Reading and Learning to Read*, 6th ed. Hillsdale, NJ: Erlbaum.

Strickland, Dorothy S., and Denny Taylor. 1989. "Family Storybook Reading: Implications for Children, Families, and Curriculum." In *Emerging Literacy: Young Children Learn to Read and Write*, edited by D. S. Strickland and L. M. Morrow, 27–34. Newark, DE: International Reading Association.

Sulzby, Elizabeth. "Children's Emergent Reading of Favorite Storybooks: A Developmental Study." *Reading Research Quarterly* 20 (1985): 458–81.

Sulzby, Elizabeth, and William Teale. 1991. "Emergent Literacy." In *Handbook of Reading Research, Vol. II*, edited by Rebecca Barr, Michael L. Kamil, Peter Mosenthal, and P. David Pearson, 727–57. White Plains, NY: Longman.

Sulzby, Elizabeth, and William Teale. 1995. "Emergent Literacy." In *The Literacy Dictionary: The Vocabulary of Reading and Writing*, edited by Theodore L. Harris and Richard E. Hodges, pp. 71–72. Newark, DE: International Reading Association.

Taylor, Denny. 1983. *Family Literacy: Young Children Learning to Read and Write.* Portsmouth, NH: Heinemann.

Voorhees, Susan. *A Wondrous World in My Head.* New York: Carney, 2013. Kindle edition.

Vygotsky, Lev S. 1978. *Mind in Society: The Development of Higher Psychological Processes.* Cambridge: Harvard University Press.

Vygotsky, Lev S. 1986. *Thought and Language* (Newly Revised). Cambridge, MA: MIT Press.

Walker, Barbara J. "The Cultivation of Student Self-efficacy in Reading and Writing." *Reading and Writing Quarterly* 19 (2003): 173–87.